CW00732484

PRECIOUS
SCARS

For Maximo and Octavia

PRECIOUS SCARS

JULIA ENGELHORN
WITH KATY WEITZ

m
B
MIRROR BOOKS

MIRROR BOOKS

© Julia Engelhorn

The rights of Julia Engelhorn to be identified as the author
of this book have been asserted, in accordance with the
Copyright, Designs and Patents Act 1988.

All rights reserved. No part of this publication may be
reproduced, stored in a retrieval system, or transmitted,
in any form or by any means without the prior written
permission of the publisher, nor be otherwise circulated in
any form of binding or cover other than that in which it is
published and without a similar condition being imposed on
the subsequent purchaser.

1

Published in Great Britain and Ireland in 2023 by
Mirror Books, a Reach PLC business.

www.mirrorbooks.co.uk
@TheMirrorBooks

Print ISBN 9781915306388
eBook ISBN 9781915306395

Typesetting: Christine Costello
Production: Chris Brereton, Simon Monk.

Printed and bound in Great Britain by
CPI Group (UK) Ltd, Croydon, CR0 4YY

Contents

Acknowledgements

I am forever grateful to my family, César, Iiro, my parents and sisters, and to my friends, who stood beside me during my worst days, who supported me and grieved with me. During and all the days after. Having you next to me has been my salvation and has helped me to put one foot in front of the other, day after day.

To my lawyers, to the policemen and woman, to all unknown people who have supported me, fought for my babies and protected me. I appreciate you for all that you have done, more than you know.

To Craig Tyson who first worked on my book, made it understandable, more coherent and fine-tuned it so I was able to find a literary agent who would take on my book. I am so thankful to you.

To Katy Weitz, you made the book what it is today. I am indebted to you. It will reach so many more people and hopefully help some of them all because of your hard work, time and your insightful questions to help me think and come to some insights I did not have before.

It is difficult to find the words to express my gratitude to so many different people who have helped me along my journey. Even before tragedy struck, everyone I have met, and not met, has made me who I am today, and therefore contributed to the book you hold in your hands. Even you, dear reader. Thank you, from the bottom of my heart.

I do believe I have been changed for the better.
And because I knew you,
I have been changed,
For good.

STEPHEN LAWRENCE SCHWARTZ,

FOR GOOD FROM WICKED

Preface

Kintsugi is the ancient Japanese art form of repairing broken pottery by mending the areas with golden glue. The philosophy behind it is to value the beauty of the broken object with its imperfections, to celebrate, not hide them. Over time, and with a lot of work, I am healing, but the scars I carry with me, inside me, are a reminder of what I have survived. From the broken pieces of my old self, something new was created, just as beautiful, but different. Everyone grieves differently, there is no right or wrong way. One might never get there, the journey of healing may take a lifetime, but every step forward is a victory, no matter how long it takes. We all carry this strength inside us.

I remember reading somewhere that parents find meaning from their tragedies. This book is my way of finding that meaning, my way of ensuring that the deaths of my twins, Maximo and Octavia, were not in vain. Something good will come of it, however small. It will never make the loss easier, but at least maybe someone, somewhere, at some point, will read this book and use it to heal and learn to live with the scars. They might even make something beautiful from them.

When a wife or husband loses their spouse, they are

widowed. When a child loses his parents, he or she is an orphan. There is no English word that describes a parent losing their child. Losing a child is against how things should be. A child buries his parents, not the other way around. Unfortunately, there are many instances where this is not the case. The world for these parents is forever changed. In Sanskrit there is a word, *vilomah*. It means "against the natural order".

***

The 6th of April 2017 was the worst day of my life.

Nothing will ever be as awful. I realised then that I had thought I was living in a bubble, and that nothing could and would harm my loved ones or me. What a fool I was. My bubble burst in the worst way possible. It takes me quite a while to even write this down. Tears keep streaming down my face, and I need to take breaks. I am numb, and I find myself staring at the screen not knowing how much time has passed.

This book is my perspective, and my opinion, on what happened to our family. I am sure his family and friends hold a different view, which is of course fine.

PART ONE
BEFORE

Mario

"My dearest Octavia and Maximo,
You have been gone longer than three months
(three months and 19 days to be exact)
and it hasn't gotten any easier for me."

LETTER ONE

It was a beautiful Tuesday morning in Cape Town.

The winter sky was clear and as is usual at this time of year, there seemed to be a glimmer over the mountains and sea and on the leaves of the trees lining the roads. The end of May always brought such a magical atmosphere. I had just finished speaking to Mario on the phone when the realisation came to me that I wanted a divorce. It was like a huge neon sign fully aglow. One thought kept going through my head – *why on earth has it taken me so long to reach this conclusion?* It was 2014, we had been married seven years. Now that I had realised what I needed to do, it was so obvious.

I walked, deep in thought, from the car park in Steenberg Village to Bodytec where I was going for an exercise session. I did not feel like going to gym but thought I should at least finish the classes I had prepaid for, otherwise Mario would get annoyed that I had wasted money. I was worried about how he would react.

Mario had been in Barcelona for the past few months. Though we had moved to South Africa over two years earlier he rarely stayed in the country longer than a month and the length between his visits had expanded over the years.

'You're spending more time in Spain than in South Africa,' I told him during the last call. 'You have three children now. It's time for you to spend more time here.'

'You're right,' he agreed. 'I'm happy you're saying this.'

Why are you happy? I thought, irritably. I thought this was always the idea from the beginning. Why would I even have to say it? Was this a test? Had he been waiting all this time for me to say something? He should *want* to be with me, to be with his family.

'I'm going to start looking for somebody to delegate the work to,' he went on.

You should have been doing that the moment we moved to Cape Town, not two and a half years later. I didn't say it.

'Okay. Good,' I replied. Then, since I was running late for my class, we ended the call. And that was when it hit me: *I don't want him here.* All this time I had waited patiently for him and now I didn't want him anymore. What I wanted was a divorce.

We had first decided to move to Cape Town in 2007, and though we had both been keen to leave Barcelona, the destination was more his idea than mine. My sister Vicky had relocated here a few years earlier with her South African husband Johan and we both fell in love with the place when we came to visit. It is a beautiful country, the people are kind and helpful, the food and the wine are excellent and, as Mario pointed out, the cost of living was far lower than in pricey Barcelona. Out here, you could enjoy a wonderful lifestyle on a far lower budget, something which appealed to him. We finally made the move in 2012 and though I had expected Mario to spend a lot of time travelling between Spain and South Africa in the beginning, I hadn't imagined he would still be living mostly in Spain nearly three years later.

Now that the realisation hit I could think of nothing else. Why had I not seen it before? I'd known for a while that we had problems. Living in different countries, let alone continents, is not a recipe for a successful marriage. But now I could see that, for me, the problems started long before the move.

The beginning of our relationship was beautiful. We met one night in July 2005 when my sister Ana and I went out to a bar in Barcelona. As soon as I walked in, I saw him. He was handsome, well-dressed with short black hair and tall. He was at least 6 ft 2 inches and towered over the other men stood next to him at the bar. These things mattered to me since I'm six foot myself and Spanish men don't often match me in height. Throughout the night my eyes kept sliding over to where he was sitting with two friends. *Why does he keep looking at me?* I wondered. *It must be because I'm constantly staring at him!* A little while later I went to the bar to order drinks and when I turned around he was there, behind me.

'Your friend told me…' he started.

I interrupted him: 'No, no, she's my girlfriend… no… my friend. I mean my *sister*.'

I was so flustered, seeing him there beside me, I could barely get my words out. We started talking and I discovered Mario was a maxillofacial surgeon, focussing on facial reconstructive surgery and implants. He seemed way out of my league, maybe because he was older and more sophisticated than my previous boyfriends. We talked about animals and he showed me a picture of his dog, a Neapolitan mastiff called Roma. She was a big dog with folds of skin hanging off her face and I thought she was beautiful! He was at the club with two others, a man and a girl. The girl, however, seemed to want more from Mario and did not look happy when he and I were chatting. We had a great night together talking and dancing. Ana eventually left, while I stayed with Mario.

From the beginning, I felt Mario was different than the other men I had dated. For one thing, he was 12 years my senior, so he seemed more mature and established in his own life. He was charming, chivalrous, and had exquisite manners – opening doors, pulling out my chair when we sat down to eat, taking me to excellent restaurants and later buying me beautiful jewellery. He paid attention to me in a way I had never experienced before, and it was flattering. Since I had always had my own money I was used to paying my own way so it was refreshing to have a boyfriend who could pick up the bill instead of going halves all the time.

We talked a lot in those early months, spending hours over dinner, getting to know one another, discussing nothing in particular. At 23 years old I was in love and after just a few months I told my friend Laura he was 'the one'. I just had a feeling.

My family seemed to like him too, which was important as we were a very close-knit clan. My father Kurt, though now based in the UK, is originally German and my mother Carmen comes from Spain. My three sisters and I had grown up in Switzerland before moving to the UK when I was 11 and though we had all scattered to different countries over the years, we remained close and got together every summer in Spain and every winter in Switzerland.

Financially, we were in a very fortunate position as my paternal grandfather Curt Engelhorn had made a considerable fortune from selling his chemical company BASF and consequently we were all beneficiaries of a family trust fund. While I was at Strathclyde University studying a Hospitality and Tourism degree my father organised work experience for me in Mexico in a large hotel resort through his contacts. I got to work in various different areas of the hotel – the cleaning department, the kitchen and the back office – over five weeks.

After my Hospitality and Tourism degree, I had no idea what I wanted to do with my life, other than knowing for certain I did not want to go into hotel management. That's when my younger sister Ana, studying in Barcelona, suggested I come to Spain.

I enrolled on a course at the university and Ana and I rented apartments one on top of the other as I tried to figure out my future direction. After about a year I met Mario and we enjoyed a glorious summer together. His dog Roma came too. I always thought that you could see what a person with a dog is like by seeing how they treat the dog and the character of the dog. And Roma was a great big cuddly teddy bear. We were once out for lunch and a little girl came out of nowhere and hugged Roma from behind. Roma didn't move a muscle, except her tail which she wagged from side to side in contentment. It was a good sign.

We dated for about a year before he proposed on a trip to Romania with my parents in 2006. At the time, I didn't know if I should accept. I was happy, so I was unsure why I was hesitant. Maybe because it was a big step. I knew he was planning to propose. He always carried a jacket around, even when it was hot. One day in the car he said he was tired of having the jacket on his lap and asked me to hold it. I was annoyed at this – *I'm not a coat hook, why can't he hang it up in the car or place it on the seat or in the boot?* Nevertheless, I placed the jacket on my lap, as he had asked, with my hands folded on top. Immediately, I felt a big ball of plastic in the pocket.

My confusion mounted. What is that? Mario was not the type of man to walk around with things bulging out of his pockets. Everything he wore was impeccable. He never even wore shorts, preferring not to show off his 'chicken legs', as he called them. I was bewildered. Without meaning to, I tightened my hands around the plastic and felt the box. It was the type of box that any woman, or person for that matter, would assume contained a ring inside. Now I was irked. *Why would he hand me the jacket with the ring inside if there*

Mario

was even the slightest possibility that I would feel it? Was this his plan, and if so, why? It didn't make any sense.

But more confusing than anything else was my own reaction. I should have been elated. I should have had butterflies in my stomach at the thought of what he planned to do. But I didn't. Not even close. Why wasn't I thrilled at the thought of getting married to this man? Over the next couple of days I tried to analyse my feelings. I had never been gung-ho about the idea of getting married, unlike my sister Vicky who always said she wanted to be married with four children at a young age. I suppose getting married just wasn't that important to me. I wasn't even sure if I wanted kids. So maybe that was the reason. On top of that, the fact that the engagement was no longer a surprise probably dampened my own enthusiasm. I loved surprises.

He proposed a few days later in the garden of a beautiful church in the village where we were staying. I don't remember what he said as I wasn't really listening, I was trying to decide what I was going to say. In the end I said 'yes' because I wasn't 100 per cent sure of what I wanted, and I thought I could always change my mind later. I also felt that it would be uncomfortable for him if I refused while we were here with my parents. I loved him, we got along well, and my family liked him. And in the end, I didn't have a good reason why I shouldn't accept so I said yes and put my apprehension down to nervousness.

The ring was beautiful. Mario had designed it himself. The diamond was held by the two opposing sides of a capital E, the first letter of my surname, and though it was too small for my finger it was stunning. The fact that he had put so much thought behind it was something I appreciated. After we returned to the hotel I told him that I would go downstairs to tell my parents and he said he had asked them already, and they knew that he was planning it. This was something else I appreciated and reminded me why I loved him. Mario was a gentleman, he was respectful, well-mannered and placed importance on these little details.

The story he told next was hilarious and summed up my father rather well. Mario went to ask for my parents' blessing in their hotel room. My mother answered the knock at the door and let him in when he asked to talk to them. She said that my father was in the bathroom and Mario turned to leave, saying he would come back later. My father, being who he is, opened the bathroom door, and while he was still sitting on the toilet told Mario he could say what he had come to say. In shock, Mario kept his composure, and looking only at my mother, told them what his intentions were. They both happily gave their consent and we had a great story to tell.

Our wedding was fantastic. We celebrated with friends and family at our family-owned restaurant El Paradiso in St. Moritz, Switzerland. Mario had left the organisation up to me, showing very little interest in the details, which I assumed was normal. After the church wedding, we went to the lift in a horse-drawn carriage and up the chair lift to be greeted at the top by five alpine horn blowers. I hadn't had so much fun in a long time. I danced on tables, drank too much and enjoyed celebrating with my new husband and friends.

Mario

The next morning I had an awful hangover. *God, I wish I hadn't agreed to drive us to the airport*, I thought as I navigated the winding roads of the Swiss Alps. But Mario had insisted on returning to work the day after the wedding and said it was too expensive to hire a driver. Besides, he said he couldn't drive because he did not know the way. Thankfully, there was no snow as it was July. Still, it was a pain and I realised too late I should have insisted that we organise a taxi.

We took a while to fall pregnant, but after a year and a half of trying, we were successful. By then I had changed my mind about children and wanted desperately to start a family with Mario. Because it took longer than we expected, the process became a big part of our life. I remember getting the pregnancy test results and waiting impatiently for Mario to come home, excited at the thought of his reaction. But when I told him I had a wonderful surprise for him, he guessed wrong. I was disappointed, but shrugged it off, thinking it was not at the top of his list. He was more concerned about getting a loan from my family so that he could invest in some real estate opportunities.

I enjoyed the pregnancy. I slept a lot – up to 10 or even 12 hours a day – craved meat all the time and went off alcohol completely. The birth went smoothly but things started to change shortly after César was born in July 2009, even though I didn't realise it at the time. Before, Mario and I would go out for long dinners at least twice a week and meet for lunches when he had the time. But now, since I wanted to be present for César, I couldn't face the late nights more than once a week. Mario, however, was keen to carry on with the same lifestyle as before the birth. He wasn't interested in changing nappies or helping to bottle feed our baby and suggested a live-in nanny to watch César while we went out together. But I found it hard to let go. And for some reason or other, the nannies never seemed to work out because Mario always found fault with them.

After our wedding, Mario's feeling for my family also changed, although this was so gradual I hardly noticed it at first. We had family meetings often and in the past, he had been an enthusiastic and active member of the family. But over time he stopped coming, saying that he needed to work. It was valid and I understood, but there were occasions where he could have been with us. César seemed to see less and less of him. Mario was never awake in the morning when I took César to pre-school. He usually arrived home late when César was already in bed or just in time to spend 30 minutes or so with him. Weekends were a bit better, but not much. I also realised that he was not as attentive to me as before. He always used to get up from the table when I did or open the car door for me. Now he seemed to do it less and less.

Still searching for my own role, I started to get more involved with our family business interests in Spain. I was very excited when, after a trip to England for a family meeting, I told him that I was going to be taking on more responsibilities for our hotel and restaurant business. It was the only time he ever came to collect me from the airport and he complained about traffic, finding a parking spot and the cost of the ticket. Then he told me that he disapproved. He said he did not understand why I wanted to become more involved. There was no need, and he did not want me to put extra miles on our car, as it would involve me driving a couple of hours a week. The discussion ended there. It was a bit of a downer but I did it anyway, though always with his disapproval.

Then, some months after the birth, Mario arrived home late and woke me, screaming in pain, saying he needed to go to the hospital in Barcelona. Fortunately we had a nanny at the time so I asked her to take care of César as I was not sure when we would be back. As I drove down to the hospital, Mario told me that he had collided with a wild boar, a nuisance in that area. The impact threw him over the handlebars of his Vespa and he landed on his shoulder.

A few minutes later a guy, also on a Vespa, stopped to help him. He offered to call an ambulance but Mario insisted on being dropped off at home. I didn't understand why he didn't go to the hospital directly, as he was in a lot of pain, wincing at every turn or when I stepped on the brakes. He said that as the boars were protected, he didn't want to pay the fine if the police found out. It didn't seem to make much sense to me, but I did not know the laws concerning boars and concentrated on trying to get to the hospital as smoothly as possible. The X-rays showed that he had a broken shoulder blade.

For a year after the accident Mario was unable to work as a maxillofacial surgeon. Fortunately, he found a buyer for his dental business and, with a loan from my family, started his investment business. It was not an inconsiderable sum, by anyone's standards, but when Mario first approached me with his plan to help people with home loans, I thought it sounded like a great idea. My trustees weren't quite as enamoured. They are responsible for all the money and assets in the family trust and it is their duty to ensure the capital is invested wisely.

'One million euros is a lot for someone with no experience in this area,' said one. 'Maybe he should start off smaller and build from there.'

But I was insistent. I knew our family had previously loaned money to start-ups as I had worked with my father's angel investment company and wanted to help my husband build a successful business. In the end the trustees agreed to loan him the money.

Mario worked with two different guys who helped him find suitable investments. But, inevitably, Mario complained that he could not find anyone trustworthy to work with, and that he had to double-check everything his right-hand man did. He also had various options of overseas investments that would require us to move there. I tried to support him by being open to where we moved but he see-sawed a lot, or at least it seemed that way to me, describing so many different options that I would lose track of what he was planning or working on. He was also unhappy about how his investments were going, and never mentioned one going well.

It was only much later that I realised he was a loan shark.

At first, when he had explained that he wanted to invest in the homes of people who could not get help from a bank, it sounded so noble, so honourable. If it weren't for Mario these people would lose their homes! But with the benefit of hindsight I understood it wasn't quite so altruistic as he made out. My trustees were a little more realistic from the start, indicating that they did not expect to see a return on their loan in the immediate future.

I assumed too, that since Mario was no longer working as a surgeon, he would be at home and able to spend more time with César. But he was always busy. Mario still went out till the early hours, he slept late and was never present in the morning. In Spain it is usual to have long lunches, and he was a master at them, so he was usually not home to see César after nursery.

When César was a year and a half, Mario missed a Christmas that we had planned to spend with my family in Switzerland. César and I had flown out first and Mario was going to meet us later as he needed to work, but the day before he was supposed to travel, he said he could not make it as he was sick. At the time it never occurred to me that he would lie. It was only much later I started to question the things he told me. César was so upset. I tried to explain to him that his father was too sick to travel. Luckily, all the presents and the company of his cousins proved a good distraction for him.

Mario did not want to live in Spain forever, as he did not like the Catalan mentality or how expensive everything was, so I knew we would live abroad. The only question was – where? For a time he played with the idea of working for the Qatari monarchy, opening a dental surgery there. He even flew out for an initial meeting with a representative of the family and returned, boasting they had offered him a blank cheque to work for them, but said it was not a place where I would be happy as it was too restrictive for European women. Again, it was only later that I wondered whether this was true. If Mario had really been offered a blank cheque I think he would have taken it.

For a while we also talked about moving to South America since he was close to investing there. We very nearly moved, but the deal was taking a long time, so we decided it would be best to move to Cape Town first and if the South American deal came off we could always relocate later. In January 2012 we packed up our belongings from our home in Spain and moved to Cape Town.

I guess I knew deep down things weren't perfect between us but I had high hopes that South Africa would be a fresh start, a chance for us to move forward together as a family.

Twins

"As you only lived for three and a half years, which is such a short time, I don't want you to be forgotten by others. I will always remember, as will the rest of the family. But is that enough? I don't know."

LETTER TWO

It must have come as a shock to family and friends when we finally moved as we had been telling them for the last five years that we were going to relocate. After spending the Christmas together in Switzerland with my family, César and I flew to Cape Town and Mario returned to Barcelona. We were taking over a family-owned house on the outskirts of town. My sister Vicky ran a hotel in the city centre and they had originally planned to use this house in conjunction with the hotel, perhaps for larger families, but it never worked out that way and it seemed perfect for us so I offered to rent it. The idea was that César and I would move first and Mario would join us after a couple of months, once we had settled in. It was hard in the beginning, being on my own and César missed his father, asking frequently: 'Where's Daddy?'

'He's in Spain,' I reply. 'He needs to work but he will come.'

We tried our best to maintain contact over Skype but it wasn't easy with the dodgy internet connection from our house, so we spoke mainly on the phone and just waited until we were together again. *That's not such a bad thing*, I told myself. *The move will do us some good, we'll appreciate each other more.*

And for a while it seemed to work.

I did miss him. Or at least I told myself I did. César was in school, and I signed up to various courses to keep myself busy. I joined the gym, saw my sister and her children at the weekends and started to make friends. I was happy. It was an exciting new chapter in our lives, a much simpler life, which I unknowingly needed. The house was a perfect size and just on the one floor, which made life with a child manageable.

Our house in Barcelona – 'El Palacete' – though beautiful, was spread out over four levels so it wasn't very practical when running around after a toddler. Our new home felt much cosier and easier to live in. The lifestyle here was also much more relaxed. You could turn up to a supermarket in bare feet and nobody would bat an eyelid. On top of that there was no need for me to go out to various late-night social engagements with Mario. I could live on César's schedule and it wasn't an issue.

I was quite happy the way things were going. Mario would come every couple of months and stay for two to three weeks at a time. It wasn't ideal but I fully expected him to make the move over to South Africa permanently within the year. In the meantime, we talked about trying for another child. Personally, I was in no hurry and didn't feel the need to expand

Twins

our little family. Mario argued that it would be better for César not to be an only child and in the end, I relented. He had a good point. I was one of four myself and couldn't imagine growing up without my siblings for company.

Once the decision was made I looked forward to having another child, though I didn't expect it to happen straight away since it had taken a while to conceive the first time. By now César was older and more independent so I would be able to give a new baby the attention it needed without César feeling too left out. For some reason I had a hunch that we were going to have twins.

I knew things weren't perfect between me and Mario but the longer I lived on my own, the more I got used to it. It was my sister who pointed it out.

'You seem happier when he's not around,' she observed. It was true. There was always so much more work when he was at home. He didn't like to use GPS and had never orientated himself so I had to drive him round everywhere, entertaining him like a house guest.

Looking after his needs meant I had to stop all my regular appointments and classes. And it wasn't like he ever helped with the chores. The one time I asked him to go to the supermarket to buy some milk he had scoffed: 'I'm not going. Supermarkets! So many people and standing in queues. How awful!'

He never cooked, he didn't clean up or even take César to the park or playground. Vicky was right. Life was easier when he wasn't around and it got to the point where I would look forward to Mario returning to Spain.

But I didn't bring this up with him. I hated to rock the boat, especially as Mario was only ever in South Africa for a short time. Besides, I was never one for confrontation. My sisters called me 'Switzerland' because I was always the neutral one in arguments. And with Mario he had a way of calling me 'little girl' which stopped me in my tracks. Whenever I made a general observation on a political issue, for example, he would look at me as if I had no clue and say condescendingly: 'Oh, my little girl!'

In Mario's mind, the daily tasks involved in looking after a child and running a household were somebody else's problems and I guess because he saw me coping he never thought I needed the help. Consequently, our issues were never discussed, never aired, and in the end we found ourselves living entirely separate lives. Still, I convinced myself that it was all fixable. *It will be different when he comes to live here permanently. Things will change then.*

By New Year's Eve 2013 I suspected that I was pregnant. We were at Vicky and Johan's for a big party with many friends. Mario didn't mingle very well. I spent most of the evening by his side so he would not be alone. I did not want to jinx it so I kept quiet. Despite my misgivings about the marriage, I still looked forward to having another child. Perhaps it was the hormones raging round my body, perhaps it was the excitement of the New Year celebrations, but I wasn't at all worried about the future. The pregnancy surely meant Mario would move permanently to South Africa and then, once he was living here, we could sort our issues out. I sipped my drink slowly and shortly after midnight we were able to head home. As César was only three, we had the perfect excuse, and I didn't have to say that I was exhausted.

Sure enough, it was confirmed not long after. Now, whatever doubts I had about our relationship I pushed to the back of my mind. The most important thing at this moment was to make sure the pregnancy went smoothly and that César was okay with the new addition. I felt that whatever problems we had were mine to fix. I was the one that had changed, not Mario. I had to find my way back to him somehow or learn to accept that this was the way things were now.

We went to see my gynaecologist Dr Penkin who showed us the ultrasound and asked: 'What do you see?'

I saw two tiny little blobs, and the shock on Mario's face.

'Twins?' I asked, shyly. As soon as we left her office, I wanted to call my mother to tell her the news but Mario urged me to wait

'Maybe we should wait before sharing the news,' he said. 'My parents don't need to know yet.'

But I was overjoyed and keen to let my mother know the outcome of the scan. She knew we were going for this scan so it would seem strange if I didn't call to tell her how it went. It's not like we had waited any time before sharing news of César's pregnancy. Twins! I always thought that it would be so great to be a twin as you would have this incredible connection with your sibling; you would always have someone with you and never be alone.

'It doesn't matter if I tell *my* parents,' I said. 'Your parents will never find out because they don't have a relationship. I will tell them, you can tell your family when you like.'

He didn't reply.

'Are you okay?' I asked.

'Yes, I'm just a bit in shock.'

I don't think he ever got over the shock that we were going to have twins.

By July 2013, I was heavily pregnant so could not fly to Spain for our annual trip to Palamos, where my family have a holiday home. But I did not want to deprive César of a summer holiday so I sent him with my sister Vicky and her four kids. The holiday was for three weeks, the longest time César would be away from me, but I made sure to speak to him on the phone as often as he wanted and for as long as his attention lasted and I felt comfortable knowing he was with my family. In South Africa he spent practically every weekend with his cousins so I knew he would be happy enough without me. And this way he got to spend time with his father at the weekends. Well, that was the plan at least. As it turned out Mario only showed up once during the entire three week trip.

I knew he was due in Palamos so when I talked to Vicky during our daily call I asked if Mario had been.

'Yes. He took a meeting with the trustees, got angry for some reason and left without seeing much of César. He didn't even stay the night.'

I was upset on César's behalf. Mario hadn't seen his son for a while, now he was right there on his doorstep and he couldn't even make the effort to spend time with him.

'How is César?' I asked Vicky.

'He's happy. He's playing with Nano. He doesn't seem to be too bothered.'

Twins

Well, if César seems fine playing with his cousin then I guess it's not the end of the world. My son was nearly four now and either he didn't realise his father had left early or was so used to not seeing him that he no longer noticed the absence. *How sad*, I reflected, *that he had become so accustomed to the situation he didn't even ask for his father anymore.* It was a shame but I felt there was nothing I could do to make Mario more connected to his son. Mario never mentioned anything to me about the trip to Palamos and I didn't bring it up either.

It was only later when I realised I wanted a divorce that incidents like this resurfaced in my mind, and I wondered why I had never talked about them with Mario. There were so many! At the time I had brushed them off, dismissing them as insignificant. Mario simply wasn't a hands-on dad, I told myself. But when I finally put these things together, they seemed like a colossal sign shouting 'Wake Up!'.

Why? Did I *purposefully* ignore all these signs? Was it a case of shutting the blinds and not allowing anything to come through? Perhaps I was just too scared to face up to the truth. I was never good with confrontation or arguments. Perhaps I could have fought harder to make Mario a better father, a better husband, to make him face his responsibilities to us and then… and then… and then what?

Would things have worked out any differently? Perhaps. Perhaps not.

The twins showed no sign of wanting to come out so on August 26, 2013, I had an appointment to be induced. That morning I drove Mario to the hospital after dropping César at school. Yes, I drove. It might sound strange now but I didn't even question it at the time. I wasn't yet in labour, after all, and Mario was unfamiliar with the route to the hospital. Before giving birth, I had tried to show him countless times how to get from our house to the hospital but he didn't seem interested. It simply never occurred to him to get himself orientated. We spent all day there waiting for the slightest contraction, but nothing happened.

Finally, I had to have a caesarean as Octavia was in distress from the cord around her neck. I would have preferred to have the babies naturally but by then, it was not an option. It was not a pleasant experience. It felt as if there was an alien inside me when the doctor had her hands in me trying to get the babies out, making me feel nauseous.

But when they came out and were handed to me, I felt they were just perfect. Maximo arrived first and then Octavia. That was wonderful as Octavia means eight and she is my parent's eighth grandchild. For a while, we discussed calling them Octavius and Maxima. At least Mario suggested it, but it just sounded strange to me. I preferred Maximo and Octavia. After the birth a nurse took us to a general waiting area while my single room was prepared.

'What is taking them so long?' Mario complained loudly. 'This is ridiculous. Why isn't your room ready now?'

'Why don't you go home and rest,' I suggested. 'When you've had a sleep you can bring César.'

I just wanted to be alone. I was tired of Mario's negative attitude and just wanted some rest. Not long after he left they took me through to my room with the babies and finally, I could gaze at them sleeping peacefully and shut my eyes.

Twins

Mario stayed for a month in Cape Town before returning to Barcelona. For the first two weeks, my mother was also at home, cooking and helping out. My parents lived in England and I only saw Mama during the holidays with the rest of the family so it was nice to have her to myself for so long. She shopped and cooked for us so that I could concentrate on the babies. But Mario wasn't happy with this arrangement, something I only found out after she left.

One day, while she was cooking and I was sitting on the sofa in the kitchen we started laughing about something. I don't even know what it was about but at that very moment Mario walked in and assumed we were laughing about him. He brooded on this for a while, then after she left he confronted me: 'I felt left out because you were paying attention to your mother, not me.'

It was a surprise to hear this.

'My mother was here to help me,' I said diplomatically. 'She has done everything from cooking to shopping. I wanted to spend time with her because I don't see her so often.'

He didn't say anything else but it irked me that he should have been thinking about himself during this period when I was just worried about looking after our twins. It wasn't like he had helped at all during this time.

Mario was not good with young babies, I knew that from our experience with César. The one time I asked him to change Maximo's nappy he screwed up his face in disgust: 'Do I have to?'

I never asked him again. But my life was now consumed by two tiny human beings and I simply didn't have time to worry about Mario's feelings. Consequently, we never talked about anything of importance like how difficult it was with the twins or that he was not changing nappies or helping. Mario assumed that we could hire all the help we needed.

It's true that I had a good helper in the form of my house-keeper Sadi Nxawe but I was reluctant to get a night nurse as I wanted to do it all myself. I was going to breastfeed them, so I didn't see the point. But Mario insisted relentlessly, which in the end I was thankful for. The nurse started the day we got back from the hospital. It was difficult in the beginning not to go and see what was happening when the twins were crying, but after a few days, I slept and only woke to feed the babies.

A few days after we arrived home, I found I was unable to carry on breastfeeding. With César, it had been painful and I ran dry after two weeks, but with the twins it was unbearable. I cried during the feeds and could not relax. I told my mother it was painful but didn't reach out for solutions and nobody offered up any remedies so finally and reluctantly, I decided to give them the bottle.

What's wrong with me? I scolded myself. *How was it I couldn't do the most natural thing a mother should be able to do?* I cried angry tears in the bathroom, furious that I couldn't stick it out, that I had somehow let them down. Now I look back and I wonder why I hadn't asked for help or even Googled to find solutions to lessen the pain, like cabbage leaves or warm wet towels on the breasts. I always assumed that the pain was something I had to endure in the early days, after which it would get more comfortable.

Twins

When the babies started on formula I could sleep through the night. Unfortunately, after a week the night nurse got sick with the flu. I hoped she would return soon but in the meantime, I slept in the babies' room to be there for them when they woke up. It didn't make much difference because Mario never slept in our bed anyway. He fell asleep most nights in front of the computer or reading in a chair so by the time he came to bed in the early hours I was always asleep. But it annoyed him that the nurse was sick. Never once did he suggest that he would look after them and that I should sleep in the bed.

At least he was spending more time with César, who was happy to hang out with his father. He was four when the twins were born and delighted at having not one but two siblings. They were the cherry on top of his ice cream and he became a real hands-on brother, helping to feed and hold one when I was busy with the other. He learnt very quickly to identify which of the twins was crying. If I was in the kitchen and heard a cry, he would say: 'Mommy, that's Octavia.' Or, 'It's Maximo.'

I could not complain to Mario that I was tired because he would have told me to get another night nurse. In retrospect, it would have been easier on me, and probably the twins and César as well. But it was difficult to leave their side. Maybe it was because of my obsession in thinking that only I could do it properly.

When they were three weeks old I had to leave them in Sadi's care to organise their papers and passports. I was only out of the house for an hour, but it felt like the longest hour of my life. Of course, they were none the wiser and were happily asleep when I returned.

Sadi was happy that I had finally reached out for her help. At first my mother had been the one I turned to but after she left I relied on Sadi as Mario was unwilling to stay with the twins alone.

'I need to go to the supermarket,' I told him one morning.

'Are you taking the twins?' he asked.

'No. I can't. They're too little…'

'Then ask Sadi to take care of them while you are out.'

Mario could have gone shopping or he could have tried to look after his own children. But he wouldn't do either. He didn't even feed them with the bottle. Now it dawned on me that I could not feed the twins during the night and be a competent mother during the day. Mario was about to leave, and I had to be there for César as well. The first night nurse had recommended a colleague so I contacted her and we hit it off straight away. She was excellent, and I was finally able to sleep through the night again.

Mario left for Spain when the babies were a month old. You'd think I would dread his leaving but again it was a relief to see him off. *That's good*, I thought as I drove him to the airport. *Now I only have to take care of three kids.* It wasn't at all good, of course, that I felt this way but I kept reminding myself that Mario had never been good with babies and that he had formed a stronger connection with César as his son got older. It would be the same with the twins, I thought.

In any case, I was totally wrapped up in their incredible world. From the moment we brought them home, I had

Twins

them sleeping together in the crib. I did not want to separate them as I thought that they would be happier knowing that the other was close. And it seemed that was true.

They always slept facing each other, breathing the same air, sharing an unseen and unknowable bond. I have countless pictures of them sleeping like that, their foreheads touching. *They'll always have each other*, I thought, as I watched them doze. Being their mother was tough but it was also a privilege, one that I never took for granted.

From the word go they had completely different personalities. Octavia was the loud one, always ready to complain, while Maximo was quieter and more reserved. I learned a lot in those early months about how to juggle two babies at the same time, like trying to carry two car seats at once. Or how to take them out of their seats – with difficulty as it turned out! The first one you can take nicely and put on your shoulder but the other you have to grab by their shoulder, one-handed, and pull them out by their arm.

It can look a bit rough from the outside but really, there's no way round it when you don't have a pram with you. It was a challenging few months – as well as a very steep learning curve – and though I knew Mario wouldn't have been much help, I did miss having someone to share the milestones with me. Those first smiles, first giggles, the first time they rolled onto their tummies. These are the moments only parents truly appreciate. I sent numerous pictures and messages but Mario didn't react much. He certainly never said that he wished he was with us.

Later that year I travelled to Switzerland for Christmas

with the kids and Sadi. They were just over three months old now and Mario was going to meet us there. He had not been back to South Africa since leaving at the end of September so César was looking forward to spending time with his father after another long absence. But in the end, Mario did not come.

He had just been appointed Honorary Consul of Macedonia in Spain. It was perfect, he said, a position that did not give him too much work while at the same time opening doors to investment opportunities and contacts. He told me he hoped for a consul licence plate and diplomatic passport so he could park anywhere and jump the airport queues. That's the sort of thing Mario enjoyed – the VIP treatment.

But another Christmas missed? That was hard to break to César. He loved his father and looked up to him, but he was already spending precious little time with him. At this stage, the excuse of work sounded terrible even to me. *No one works during Christmas. Everyone is on holiday.* I knew it was a long way to travel for a couple of days, but Christmas was one of the most magical days for kids and this would be the first with our twins.

I tried to put Mario's absence to the back of my mind while we decorated the tree and hid the presents for the kids but felt a niggling discomfort as, once again, I watched my son open his presents without his father. I resolved to talk to Mario about the situation when we flew to Spain at the start of the new year to spend time with his family for Three Kings Day, a Spanish holiday that some families celebrate more than Christmas.

Twins

I needed to know what was going on. As long as the grand-parents were alive and the grandchildren young, I felt it was important to establish a bond between them. When I was little, we had lost that connection too early and never really recovered it.

My maternal grandmother had died when I was very young and my memories of her were vague. We had little contact with my grandfather. Meanwhile, my father's mother died due to childbirth complications, and he didn't have much contact with his father Curt as he was growing up. It was only later in life that they started to communicate better and see each other more. Then, we were able to spend time getting to know our grandfather Curt and step-grandmother Heidi but by then we were older and had our own lives.

As a child I hadn't really known grandparents and I didn't want the same for my children. Family was important to me and until now I thought it was important to Mario too. But as time went on his actions told a different story.

If Mario didn't feel the same I needed to know.

Divorce

"I have just remembered that the first Christmas
without you is coming up. That will be tough to take.
I hadn't thought so far ahead.
I just try to take one step at a time."
LETTER FOUR

Mario was at the airport when we arrived in Barcelona. I assumed he had come to escort us all back to the hotel, but he had other ideas.

'I'd like to take César to El Palacete first to give him a Christmas present,' he said. 'So maybe you can get a taxi to the hotel with the twins and we'll meet you there?'

This is not ideal, I thought irritably. *Why couldn't he have brought the gift with him to the airport?* We were spending a few days with Mario's family for Three Kings Day. Unfortunately we couldn't stay longer as Mario had to return to work. To cut down on unnecessary journeys during our short visit we had decided to stay at a hotel close to Mario's parents in Mataro rather than at our home in Barcelona, which was at least half an hour's drive away. Mario looked at me expectantly. Well, what could I do?

Divorce

'Of course, take César,' I said. 'And why don't you take Sadi too? Then she can see something of Barcelona while she is here.'

As it was Sadi's first trip outside of South Africa I felt a certain responsibility for her wellbeing. *It would be nice for her to get a view of Barcelona while she is here.* But I really needed to get to the hotel in order to feed and change the twins.

They shouldn't be too far behind me if Mario only needs to give César a present, I thought as I fixed the car seats into the taxi at the airport. But Sadi called two hours later to say that they had been held up at the house and were not yet on their way to the hotel. I told her not to worry, too preoccupied with twins to notice that they were gone for several hours.

Only later did it occur to me that when César returned, he had no present with him. I didn't want to ask him about it in case he had never been given anything. And it never crossed my mind to ask Mario or Sadi.

The next few days flew by in a whirlwind of activity. It was lovely to spend time with Mario's parents, who doted over Octavia and Maximo, and some old friends dropped into the hotel to meet the twins and catch up. However, between entertaining visitors and looking after the kids it was non-stop and there just didn't seem to be a moment that Mario and I were alone together.

Before I knew it we were packing our bags for our return flights to South Africa and I never got a chance to bring up the fact that he had missed Christmas for a second time. In the back of my mind I knew that something was very wrong between us and perhaps I was avoiding confronting the issue. After all, we hadn't been intimate since we conceived the twins and there was now so much distance between us I hardly knew where to start. I was bringing up our three children on my own and for that alone I should have been furious with him. But I wasn't. I really wasn't. I guess that by this point my own feelings had changed.

Once home, the weeks sped by so quickly. Suddenly Maximo and Octavia were crawling everywhere, exploring the house and garden. They especially liked crawling on top of O'Brian, my Irish Wolfhound, and taking out fistfuls of his hair. He was most obliging and never moved a muscle. César loved playing with them, especially during bath time. He would show them how to splash the water and make them laugh. At the end of each bath session, the floor was slippery with water. For every milestone, Octavia was always two weeks ahead of Maximo. It took him a while to catch up, but he did so quickly. Maximo needed to see her do it a few times before he got it, but when he did, it was like they had both started at the same time. She was the more adventurous, he the more cautious one.

By March they were just starting to sit up, though Octavia was more stable than Maximo. He wobbled around, pitching forward, though never quite hitting his head, then pulled himself upright again. I'm not sure if he did it on purpose but this had both of them in stitches. *God, they're adorable*, I thought as I watched them having fun together, making each other laugh. It was so wonderful to be in their company and I tried to capture these special moments on camera to send to Mario so that he could share them too. I deeply regretted that he was missing so much of this incredible time in their childhood.

At the end of March, Mario was due to meet us for a family holiday but he cancelled at the last moment. By now we hadn't seen him for three months, though if César was upset about this he never let on. I think that at some stage César accepted that his father simply wasn't around anymore. He didn't ask when he was coming to visit or ask if they could talk on the phone. That broke my heart. It must have affected him but he stopped saying anything about it.

Funnily enough, I was not the first one to mention divorce. From the beginning of the year, I had been asking Mario to sign some papers for the kids in front of a notary in Spain so that their forms for residency in South Africa would be in order. They needed residency to be able to go to school in South Africa, and also to travel out of the country. But whenever I brought it up Mario maintained that his notary was very busy and that he would get around to it eventually. He never did. One day in the car park outside César's school, I was on the phone to Mario when I asked about the papers yet again.

'Hmmm… so what happens if I sign the residency papers, and you then divorce me?' he said. 'Then I would lose all my rights to the kids.'

What? What is he talking about? I was shocked.

'Signing residency papers doesn't mean you're giving your parental rights away. They need residency to go to school here,' I explained. *Why even mention divorce?* Until now I hadn't thought about divorce. Now I got nervous and I couldn't figure out why. Maybe subconsciously I knew what I needed to do, I just hadn't realised it yet.

I flew to Italy for my grandfather's birthday at the beginning of May. It was great to be able to spend more time with him and the rest of the family. Mario, of course, did not come. He was too busy with work. It was my step-grandmother Heidi who realised something was not right. One night she sat me down in the bar at the hotel and asked point blank: 'Do you still love Mario?'

I gave her such a long and complicated answer that my faith in what I was saying literally drained away as I spoke. Then, it hit me. *No, I don't love him anymore and I hadn't in a long time.* It was amazing that she, with such a simple question, could pry open the door, nailed shut and rusted, to my emotions. A flicker of light now shone through that door.

After I finished babbling, she gave me a look that said I was fooling myself. But she didn't say a word. She didn't need to. For too long I had avoided having difficult conversations with Mario.

Why hadn't he made the move with us to South Africa? Why wasn't he spending time with us at Christmas? We hadn't slept together since the conception of the twins, but it was more than that. We didn't *talk* as we had before. I knew that many marriages hit dry spells, especially after children, but we didn't seem to connect on any level. I wondered now how he felt, whether he too knew there was something wrong. *There is no alternative, I need to face this.*

A couple of weeks later, back in South Africa, we had the call when I told him he needed to be in Cape Town. And that's when I was struck by the realisation that I didn't want him to come to South Africa. All I could think about now was divorce and I knew that no amount of couples counselling would help. *I'll be in Spain for the holidays next month*, I told myself, *we can talk about it then*. Meanwhile, I started to plan what to say, writing it all down to make sure I put it clearly and without drama. But in the end it happened in the worst way possible.

The problem was, I stopped calling him. It wasn't deliberate, I just needed distance. I needed to think things through and I couldn't maintain the deception that everything was fine when things definitely weren't. I still sent pictures of the kids but since I was always the one who called him – and never the other way round – he noticed my lack of communication. Two weeks later he messaged, asking to Skype. The WiFi was terrible, there was no video and we just barely managed to hear one another.

'I know that something's wrong,' he started. 'You haven't been calling and I want to know what's bothering you.'

'Let's wait until I come to Spain in a few weeks and we can talk face to face then,' I said. I really didn't want to tell him over Skype.

'No, that's too far away. I need to know now, Julia. What's up?'

My heart drummed hard in my chest and my breathing felt shallow and unsteady. Still, I didn't say a word.

'Talk to me,' he insisted. 'Come on, Julia. You can't make me wait for two weeks. What is it?'

'I want a divorce.'

Silence. My heart was in my mouth. I had no idea what he would say next.

'Divorce? Why? Where is this coming from?' he seemed genuinely surprised.

'Well, I think I started to realise I had changed after César was born,' I explained. It helped that I had written down what I wanted to say, just to get my thoughts in order, though I didn't refer to my notes now. 'I thought it was all me so I never mentioned anything and just thought I needed to find my way back to you again so we could continue together. I thought the move to South Africa would help us – absence makes the heart grow fonder, they say – and in the beginning it did. But then after a while it didn't help at all and you never came. And I got used to doing things on my own.'

'This is… it's… it's out of the blue,' he said, seemingly shocked by my words.

I was baffled. How could this possibly be a surprise to him? We didn't live together, we didn't talk much and we weren't physically intimate. I don't know in what way he thought this resembled a normal relationship. But I didn't say this. Instead, I explained, as calmly as I could, that the distance had made it difficult for us to remain emotionally close.

I shook now as I recounted some of the things that had become apparent to me over the last few years. He listened calmly to everything I had to say. Neither of us cried. At the end of the conversation, he made a strange remark about his health, but my mind was reeling so it didn't really register. Instead we ended the call with an agreement that we would talk again the next day after he had time to digest what I had said. I put down the phone slightly in shock and guilty for not having been able to wait until we were in Spain. It only occurred to me later that night that he had not at any point tried to dissuade me from my decision. He didn't say he still loved me and he didn't suggest couples counselling.

I had an appointment with Sam the next day. She is an angel and tarot card reader as well as a Reiki healer. Getting an appointment to see her usually took weeks, but it always ended up being exactly when I needed her most. On the way, I told Vicky that I would be around later to tell her something. Sam was standing at the door of her house when I arrived and no sooner had I walked through the front gates than she announced: 'You need to get a divorce. Your and Mario's paths are separate. I'm sorry, Julia. I feel uncomfortable telling you this but it needed to be said. The cards told me that the marriage is at an end.'

'Wow,' I said. 'You're not going to believe this but I told Mario last night that I want a divorce.'

'It's the right thing,' she said. It was reassuring to hear that Sam had received this message at the same time as I had come to my decision.

Everything after that day showed me that I was right to do what I did and that I had been blind to who my husband had turned into since I had moved to Cape Town. Or maybe he was always like that, I just hadn't seen it. Long buried memories now resurfaced and all the behaviour I had excused and ignored for years now struck me with their full force. It was like waking up after a very long and deep sleep.

Vicky was shocked when I told her later that afternoon.

'My God, why did you never say anything?' she asked. 'I knew that things weren't great between you but I had no idea things were this bad.'

'I didn't realise it myself, Vicky. I kept telling myself we would sort things out eventually but that time never came and then I realised it was too late.'

By now I felt quite calm and a little relieved that it was at least out in the open.

The following day Mario and I spent two hours on the phone. It was the longest conversation we had had in months. At the end he made another cryptic comment about his health.

'What's wrong with your health?' I asked.

'Well, now that I know you don't love me I'll tell you. You know I have had these fainting fits before? I went for some tests and discovered I suffer with brain aneurysms. They're quite big and I've been told they could rupture at any time. I could be dead by next week, but it doesn't matter now because you don't love me.'

'What? That's a stupid thing to say, Mario. Of course it matters!'

'I probably won't even make it to the end of the year, so you'll be lucky. You won't even have to divorce me.'

'Don't say that!' I hardly knew how to react. Of course I was worried for him and didn't want him to die. Mario was the father of my children and they loved and needed him.

'Look, all I ask is that we wait three months to tell anyone about divorce,' he said. 'I need time to get my mind round it and figure things out.'

Divorce

'Sure,' I agreed. I was in no hurry and I certainly didn't want to put him under any more stress. I had just landed a massive bomb on him and he needed time to get used to the idea of a divorce.

I was aware that Mario had fainted a few times before. Once, not long after our move out to South Africa I nearly fell over him in the bedroom. It was one of the rare times he had gone to bed before me. The bedroom was dark and I tripped over him lying on the floor. He didn't know how long he had been passed out but he seemed fine afterwards.

'It's nothing,' he assured me at the time. 'Just stress.'

He said he had seen a doctor about it and all was well. I assumed that if there was anything more he would have told me at the time. It did hurt to think he had not trusted me enough to tell me about the brain aneurysms before now. In my opinion, you do not protect a loved one from something like that when you can die at any moment.

But then I had never told him how I felt about our marriage. It just showed how much distance there was between us. It never occurred to me, not for one minute, that he wasn't telling the truth. Mario was a doctor himself. He wouldn't lie about something like this.

Now that the floodgates were open, I started to remember more incidents from the past that I had forgotten about, incidents that, when put together, showed I should have seen this coming a long time ago. One time, before our engagement, we were in the coastal town of Mataro in my mother's car. He was trying to sell his car so while he talked to the dealer, I went to fill up with petrol. The dealership was right next to a little roundabout with a traffic light system. The lights turned from red to yellow, and I moved off, not realising that the yellow was flashing. As I joined the round-about a policeman on his motorbike had to slow down and break slightly to let me pass. I took the first exit and parked next to him. I got out to talk to the officer who had followed to give me a ticket.

'I'm sorry, I didn't realise it was a flashing orange light,' I said immediately.

'Yeah, I wouldn't normally have stopped you but I had to do an emergency stop so I really have no choice...'

'Of course, it's fine,' I smiled.

Mario, meanwhile, had come out of the dealership. He had obviously seen what had happened and seemed really upset with me. As the officer drove off he said snidely: 'You probably don't even realise what you have done!'

Why he was so annoyed? It was not his car, and I was paying for the ticket. It really wasn't a big deal. Even the police officer was reluctant to book me for such a minor infraction.

Mario had overreacted and behaved unsympathetically. I had a fleeting thought then: *do I want to be with someone like this?* It was such a small and seemingly insignificant incident I forgot about it for years but now recollections like this came back to me.

Over the next couple of weeks Mario and I spoke more than ever. At least now the truth was out in the open. It could take some time but Mario had reacted better than I'd hoped and I felt cautiously optimistic that we could come to an amicable arrangement. It wasn't such a bad idea to wait before telling other people about our divorce. That way we could talk in peace, without interference.

My sister Ana had just been through a divorce and from all accounts it seemed to have been fairly smooth and relatively pain-free. They had reached a speedy agreement and were now good friends. I hoped Mario and I could do the same. Since I was the one asking for a divorce I resolved to be as accommodating as possible. After all we would be bound together for the rest of our lives and I feared the cost to all of us if we made this difficult for each other.

Above all, I wanted the children to maintain a good relationship with their father and was confident that, with the right attitude, we could make this work.

Negotiations

"There have been a couple of good days, but deep inside there is always something missing."

LETTER FIVE

In June 2014 I flew with the kids and Sadi to Spain for the twins' baptism. They were not walking yet so at least we didn't have to run up and down the aisles after them, but they were very curious about the new surroundings. I was worried the noise in the cabin would wake them, but they slept well. Apart from confiding in Vicky, Mario and I hadn't told our families about the divorce yet as we were trying to work the arrangements first. But he was not planning to come to Palamos until the day of the baptism itself and we needed to sign some papers in advance. Thinking this was just a small formality, I signed for him. I didn't think it was a big deal but when Mario found out he was furious. I later realised that he was so angry because he realised I could fake his signature and had done so.

Still, we had a fantastic baptism at our family home up in the mountains around Palamos, with its distant views of the ocean and beautiful flowers, vineyards and olive trees. There is a tiny church attached to the *masia*, a type of farmhouse common to the Catalan countries, and the priest from the village came to perform the small and intimate ceremony, with Mario joining us for the day.

Even though we hadn't yet told our families about the divorce, Mario didn't invite his family to the ceremony, which I found upsetting. The twins' grandparents saw them little enough as it was. I tried to convince Mario that their absence looked suspicious, but he would not change his mind.

My own family *did* suspect something was wrong. Mario barely spent any time with us in Palamos and never stayed the night. And it looked odd that nobody from his family was attending the baptism. One day, while we were in the car driving down the mountain, my mother asked me directly: 'Is there something wrong between you and Mario? We don't see him anymore.'

I couldn't lie.

'No, Mama, things are not good,' I sighed. 'I've known for a while now but we talked about it last month and agreed to a divorce.' It was a relief to finally get it out in the open.

'A divorce? Oh Julia, I'm so sorry. And I'm sorry you have been unhappy. Why haven't you said anything before now?'

'I… erm… I don't know…' *Why hadn't I said anything?* Perhaps I didn't want to worry them. What could they do from so far away?

'I just felt I needed to figure it out on my own,' I said. 'And now Mario doesn't want us to tell our families because he thought it best we sort the arrangements out between us first.'

'Well, you can *always* talk to us,' Mama said firmly. 'We are your family. We are here for you.'

That was good to hear. No one in my family was surprised about the situation with me and Mario. In fact, they appeared happy that I had finally arrived at a decision. I was a bit surprised myself, thinking perhaps they would try to talk me out of a divorce. But then again, if I had been more open, they might have felt more comfortable sharing their own view.

The holiday in Spain had been nice, although Mario had not shown much interest in seeing the kids apart from taking César for one night. But I was, as ever, optimistic that we could reach an agreement regarding the children without involving the courts. César started school again in July, so Mario came to South Africa a few weeks later in August, staying with us for six weeks.

Now the twins were getting busier and busier, enjoying opening drawers and cupboards together, a new-found skill of theirs. Their favourite cupboard was where the pot and pans were kept. They made such a racket that it would bring them to fits of laughter. They also took a great interest in playing with César's toys, which mostly consisted of breaking his Lego and putting the pieces in their mouths.

During this time, the twins had their first birthday. Mario was here to celebrate it with us. I organised two giant Mickey and Minnie Mouse balloons, which fascinated them. They were a bit overwhelmed with the presents and the attention, but still enjoyed the day.

During that visit Mario slept in his office, as he had always done. We hardly ever slept together as he always said he had insomnia. Usually, he would fall asleep on the couch or come to bed when I got up. We spent a lot of time talking and getting along quite well during this time.

There were some ups and downs, but nothing major. We had not told César anything yet, and Mario wanted to keep it like that for a while. I disagreed and felt that as Mario was there with us it would be best to discuss it when we were all together. But it was something we had to do as a couple, so I gave in. I should have fought harder in that respect, but looking back, in the grand scheme of things it didn't matter. César was happy to have his father at home and I didn't want to ruin it.

On the days I had to go out, I assumed Mario spent at least some of the time with the twins. I always thought that the reason he was not around was because he did not want to spend much more time with me than needed. One day I asked Sadi whether Mario gave them attention when I was out.

'No,' she said. 'He's always up in his office'. She did not know about our divorce plans at this time and seemed a bit annoyed that Mario was too busy to spend time with his kids. I should have asked him but again, I didn't want to rock the boat. He spent most afternoons with César when he came home from school, which he loved. The twins were also happy that he was present, although they mostly played among themselves, with Sadi, our gardener Moses, or with our ever-patient dogs: O'Brian, Skollie and Koenig (our two Rottweilers) and Donatella, a Bullmastiff.

During this time we talked about the future and agreed that the kids would stay with me, they would have residency in South Africa, and I would pay for Mario's visits. He would be able to stay at the house when he was here, and I would travel to Europe with the children so he could spend time with them over their holidays.

Financially, things were quite straightforward. I had bought El Palacete so it was owned by my trust. He had no financial interest in it. Since I had my own income I never asked him for money to support the children and we kept all our accounts separate except that when Mario had sold his dental business he had requested the money be transferred into my bank account – I think it was for tax reasons.

El Palacete is a beautiful neoclassic little 'palace' from the 19th Century. Its ceilings are high with an astounding view to Barcelona and the ocean. The main floor has old black and white tiles, the others are bleached white wooden floors.

It is peaceful up there but within 30 minutes one can be in the centre of Barcelona. It is located in a little village where we have the basic amenities and has a Funicular that connects to the metro line below. It makes it very easy to get around without needing a car. In the past it was used as a *Relais & Chateaux* and to host small events. We have done a few photo-shoots here, which have been very interesting to watch, if a little disruptive.

I owed him money, he said, for improvements that he had made to the El Palacete. It was surprising he should be asking for money when he lived in the property for free without making any contribution to the utility bills. Nevertheless, if this was what it took to have an amicable divorce for the sake of the kids then I was happy to accommodate his requests.

We seemed to have reached some basic agreements and I was pleased with our progress. When Mario asked if I would travel with César to Spain so that they could spend some time together during the September holiday, I didn't think hard about it. I didn't question why he did not spend more time with the twins, or why he only wanted César to come to Spain. I just assumed that they were at a difficult age and that he would not be able to handle them on his own. I could not blame him as they were still so young and I had more experience. *He'll be better with them when they are a little older, just like with César.*

One night, just before Mario left for Spain, I was making Spätzli with bacon for the kids when he came into the kitchen holding a poorly photocopied letter. He had crossed out the name of the doctor and the hospital, but I recognised the logo on the letterhead. It stated that Mario was unlikely to survive to the end of 2014 due to numerous brain aneurysms.

'I've managed to convince my doctor friend to keep this secret,' he said solemnly. 'No one knows. He's even deleted me off the hospital records.'

'Why?' I didn't understand why he wanted to keep it so classified, especially as he was not practising medicine anymore.

'I don't want to worry my family.'

Mario's family were in medicine – his father was a gynae-cologist, his mother worked as his nurse and Mario's older brother Juan was a psychiatrist.

'You know, they might hear it from one source or another,' he went on. 'That's why I had to take it off the records. But here, you can read it.'

I looked over the letter, then handed it back and Mario walked purposely into the garden. He then made a big show of burning the paper in the garden, lighting it where I could see it out of the kitchen window while I was cooking.

We had talked about his illness before, but never at length, and up until then always over the phone. Now, for the first time, I started to doubt him. It just seemed so over the top, so calculated. But at the same time, I could not believe that he would tell such an enormous lie. And for what purpose? He would have been proven wrong in the end.

'You should talk to someone about this,' I said later that night. 'Even if you don't want to worry your family, it will help to have someone listen and give support.'

'You are the only person I've told,' he said. 'And you are divorcing me and making my life more difficult, more painful and awful.'

That was even more reason for him to talk to someone, I thought, but it seemed he was determined to keep it to himself so I put the 'illness' to the back of my mind. Whatever the truth of the matter, there was nothing I could do about it. Certainly, nobody else believed it.

My sister Vicky was sceptical from the beginning and later, when I told my trustees and the divorce lawyer they all shook their heads in disbelief. At the time I just couldn't understand it. Perhaps I was being naïve but I just didn't see the point of the lie.

Negotiations

I was feeling fairly optimistic when I arrived with César in Barcelona for two weeks in September. I had decided to leave the twins with Sadi in South Africa during this trip as I didn't think they needed any more disruption to their routine. It was hard to leave them, knowing that I wouldn't see them for the next fortnight, but I felt confident they were in good hands.

On the basis of our agreement in South Africa, I had spoken to my lawyers in Spain and they had drawn up the divorce papers in advance. The plan was to finalise details and sign the papers while I was in Spain. Mario collected César from my sister Ana's flat a day after we landed and the plan was he would have him for two weeks alone. I met with Mario and Josep, our family lawyer, someone Mario liked and respected, to talk about what we had agreed on in South Africa.

We started to go through the papers together but on page two, Mario saw something he disagreed with and refused to move on. We argued for an hour without reaching any conclusion, never moving beyond page two. It left me exhausted, depressed and feeling deceived and stupid. At the end of the meeting, Mario said he would look for his own lawyer and would be in touch once he had found someone. 'Then we can meet again to discuss this,' he concluded.

Josep seemed worried as I left. I walked out of the office in tears. Once I was a bit calmer, I called my mother to tell her how badly it had gone. She was not surprised. And neither was anyone else. It seems I was the only one who thought we would be able to reach a swift agreement.

The next day I flew with Ana and her daughter Lola for a five day holiday together in Switzerland. It was nice to have some time to myself for a change.

Since I was more or less bringing up the children as a single parent, they took up most of my time and attention while I was in South Africa. Now, though I missed them desperately, I also appreciated spending time with my sister and niece. Nevertheless, Mario's behaviour played on my mind, injecting the holiday with an undercurrent of unease.

Before arriving in Spain I assumed we had worked out the difficult stuff so the paperwork would be a fairly smooth process. Now I reminded myself that divorce was a messy business and we had only just started. Yes, it would be more difficult than I had hoped and imagined, but not many divorces ended well, especially when kids were involved.

The day I returned to Spain, I got a message from Tomeq, our Spanish gardener, saying that he wanted to meet with me. That was strange. I had not been in contact with him and Agnieska, his partner and our housekeeper, regularly since the move. I agreed and arranged to meet him in a few days' time.

In the meantime, I had to take care of some admin. South Africa had just made it a new requirement that when a parent travelled alone with their children, that parent needed written approval of the parent not present. I had told Mario that I would need a letter signed by him allowing me to travel with César to return to Cape Town. Now I reminded him of the letter.

A day later I called to speak to César and to confirm the

arrangements for the handover and that's when Mario told me I could come and fetch César, but that he would not sign any papers. It was like someone had poured a bucket of ice over my head. My whole body froze. I went completely rigid. For a moment, I did not know what to think. *If Mario doesn't give me the letter then I can't leave the country with César... and I can't get home to the twins.* Dazed, I looked out at the street from my sister's flat as cars moved up and down the road; the noise of the traffic slowly penetrated my confused mind. *Why was he making things so difficult for me?*

I sat down and thought hard. I had César's birth certificate and passport with me, and if push came to shove, I knew I could fake Mario's signature. As long as I had César I would figure it out from there. Then, if Mario asked, I could tell him they didn't ask to see the papers at the border.

It made me incredibly nervous to think about going to such extreme lengths, but if it meant that I could get home and be with all three kids, so be it. Once I had calmed down a little, I called my divorce lawyer and told her of the situation. I also told them of Tomeq's message about wanting to meet me. She asked me to come to the office to talk things through.

Next I called my family to discuss this new turn of events. Vicky said South Africa had delayed the implementation of the law as so many people had complained about it. They had tried to implement something that nobody, not even the border authorities, were ready for. I was extremely relieved. Meanwhile, no one in the family seemed surprised by Mario's actions. While I always had faith that things would work out, many had expressed concern about his intentions.

'Just be careful,' I was warned. 'Don't let your guard down. He might be telling you one thing and planning something else entirely.' To them, the 'fatal aneurysms' had been a red flag.

Now Mario kept changing his mind about whether he preferred me to fetch César or to meet at the airport. One day he sent me a message saying that he would like to bring César to Ana's apartment and not have to say goodbye at the airport, which was fine by me. The next day he said he would bring him to the airport. I said okay. He then asked if I was planning to leave without the signed paper. That's when I made a big mistake. I told him that the government had delayed the implementation of the new law and that it was not necessary. I didn't think twice about it. Even then, I couldn't see that he did not want me to leave the country.

Two days before we were due to fly home I was walking down the Avinguda Diagonal in Barcelona with my sister Ana, her daughter Lola and their dog Fortuna when I got a call on my mobile. The noise from traffic and roadworks was deafening so I held my phone closer to my ear.

'What did you say, honey? Are you having fun?' I could hardly hear my five-year-old son's reply. His tone was happy, at least.

'What was that? Can you repeat that? I couldn't hear you.'

'Oh, Mommy, I said that I will see you when you have the twins!'

WHAT!? What was Mario putting into his head? Suddenly Mario was on the line, bombarding me with questions about why my lawyers had not been in contact with him.

'But you said the last time we met that you would get a lawyer,' I replied, confused. 'We were waiting on you to get one so we could start negotiating.'

'You are wasting time, planning something with your group of lawyers, while I am on my own and having to think on my own,' he shot back. He vented a while longer and then hung up. I felt nervous and unsure of what would happen next.

In the beginning, I had felt sorry for him and listened endlessly to his complaints, his scheming, and his negativity. I'd learnt over time that it was better not to react or rise to his provocations. But that didn't always work. He had a knack of getting under my skin. Now I felt on shaky ground with Mario changing his mind all the time.

Everything felt so fragile and uncertain. César and I were due to return to South Africa in a couple of days so that he could go back to school, and more importantly, so I could be with the twins again. I had never been away from them this long.

I sent Mario a message when I got back to the apartment to confirm the details about the meet-up at the airport. He messaged back, saying he wanted to talk. My heart rate picked up a notch. I called him.

'You can forget it,' he said coolly. 'I'm not bringing César to you. I'm furious that you haven't tried to arrange another meeting with the lawyers. You can come and see César, but I won't let you take him back to South Africa. Not till we get this sorted.'

'I don't understand, Mario. You said you would come back to us once you had found a lawyer.'

'Yes, and I need more time.'

'Okay, have time, but what does it matter if I am in Barcelona or not? I need to get back to the twins.'

'I'm not stopping you going back to the twins.'

By the time we hung up I was a wreck. *Maybe I should just go to the house to collect César… No. Knowing Mario he will dig his heels in, the police will be called and there will be a terrible scene, all in front of César. That won't solve anything.*

I felt like such a fool. All the time my family and friends had warned me that Mario was not to be trusted, and I hadn't believed any of them. Now it was happening. I called my Spanish lawyer and told her that Mario was holding César, refusing to let him go.

'Okay, we'll send a private detective to watch the house to make sure César is there,' she said. 'Then he'll follow Mario if he leaves with your son.'

'A private detective? Is that really necessary?' It sounded so drastic.

'Julia, we don't know what he is planning.'

'Yes, but you don't think he's going to take him somewhere, do you?'

'He is holding your child against your will. I'm really not sure what he will do next.'

She was right. At this point I didn't know what Mario's intentions were and since I had misjudged him so often, I decided to allow the lawyer's suggested course of action.

While I was at the lawyer's office changing my flights, Vicky called with terrible news. Sadi's nephew had been killed in a knife attack in Khayelitsha, a township in Cape Town, and she needed to be with her family urgently. That meant I had to get back home as soon as possible to allow her to leave.

I called Mario to let him know and to ask if he had a lawyer we could talk to. When I told him about Sadi's nephew he didn't believe me and claimed it was a lie to get him to deliver César. He would not budge and kept repeating that he needed more time. When I asked him how much, he would not say. We were in an impossible situation. Mario refused to return César until we had a meeting arranged and we couldn't arrange a meeting unless he had a lawyer, which he seemed in no hurry to find.

I left my lawyer's office in a daze. She assured me she would call with any news. I spent the rest of the day walking aimlessly, trying to keep my mind off what had happened. That didn't work. Walking got me thinking and crying. It was a busy part of the city, with many people passing by with kids and dogs in tow.

I felt self-conscious, so I bought some sunglasses so I could avoid strange looks. I never wore those glasses again. I had my phone in my hand the whole time, checking it endlessly for news. That night I couldn't sleep. I tossed and turned, my mind going around in endless loops. *What's Mario's plan? What does he want? When will I be able to see my son or the twins? I felt so helpless, so out of control. After all my efforts and goodwill, Mario had pulled the rug from under my feet. Now it felt as if I was falling, falling, falling… and I had no idea where I would land.*

The next day I had another meeting with my divorce lawyer. Soon after I arrived, Josep called to say that the detective had just informed him that César had left the house with Tomeq and his girlfriend Agnieszka. He was following them to see where they were taking him. When Josep called back it was to say Tomeq and Agnieszka had taken César to their home.

My lawyers said legally they had to advise me not to do anything, but as they were parents themselves, they understood that I wanted to go and fetch César. I hesitated a moment, realising I was about to do what Mario had done – kidnap our son – but he left me with no choice. I was terrified that if I didn't go and take him back I would not see him for a long time.

Five minutes later, I left with one of the lawyers in a taxi to the address. We arrived at a small building with five flats or so and pressed the buttons randomly until Tomeq answered. He was surprised to see me but let me in. I was so excited to see César. He was happily watching TV and oblivious to anything that was happening. I was pleased about that. Tomeq and I were supposed to meet later that day so we sat down now and talked.

'I wanted to speak to you because Mario has told us about the divorce,' he started. 'And for a while now we have noticed that, being on his own, Mario seems to have changed. He is more distant and secretive, his moods change easily. At first we assumed that he missed you and the children, but recently we think he has a night visitor.'

I listened with interest as Tomeq explained that Mario had changed the settings on the security cameras, which he installed soon after our move to Cape Town. Before, they recorded every week, but he changed that to a 24-hour loop, meaning that whatever was recorded was wiped within 24 hours. Tomeq then said that Mario had told him the previous day not to allow me to enter the house if I showed up, and not to allow me to see César.

'Agnieska is no longer comfortable working for Mario,' he said. 'She's scared. She doesn't want to be at the house and so we want to ask you if you could let us go. Agnieska doesn't want to upset Mario by quitting. Please, you are our employer. We would like to leave.'

'Of course,' I said quickly. 'Of course you can leave. I don't want you to feel unsafe. I'll help in any way possible.'

This was a lot to process in one go.

So it seemed that Mario had a girlfriend. I didn't care about that, not one bit. More worrying were the mood swings. Why was Agnieska scared? I tried to find out but she wouldn't articulate any further. Since I took care of all the household expenses, including their wages, I assured them that they could leave at any time and that was fine by me. Now I told them that I intended to take César so that we could leave the country and return to the twins. But would they get into trouble with Mario?

'Don't worry,' said Tomeq. 'I'll tell Mario that since you are the mother I have no legal right to prevent you.'

I felt overwhelming gratitude towards Tomeq at that moment – not only was he on my side but he also appeared to have a better grasp of the situation than I did.

He assured me he wouldn't say anything to Mario until the next day. We talked a little more, and then I left with César and the lawyer for Ana's apartment to pack. There was no time to lose. I threw everything in as quickly as I could. César didn't have enough time to sit down before I told him that we were leaving again.

It was a nerve-wracking taxi ride to the airport as I was worried Mario might follow us and demand César back. At the ticket office I asked for seats on the first flight to England. There were no direct flights to Cape Town from Barcelona and all I wanted right now was to get out of Spain. I must have looked quite desperate because the woman behind the desk seemed to realise something was up, and in no time I had two tickets. César was a real trooper.

He only had an overnight bag with him. Most of his things were still at the house with his father but he never complained or even asked where his father was. If he knew something was wrong he never let on. I was so worried Mario would find out and show up at the airport or have us stopped at border control through his political contacts at the consulate. It was only when the plane trundled along the runway and rose into the air that I finally breathed properly again.

We arrived safely in England and were warmly welcomed by a relieved set of grandparents. We stayed the night at my parents' home where César had a restless night, waking frequently. In the end I crawled into bed with him and he finally seemed to relax when we curled up together.

By mid-morning the next day I had countless missed calls from Mario. I didn't pick up. I couldn't risk giving away my location. It was only when we were back in Cape Town a day later that I talked to him. By then he had calmed down and said he couldn't really blame me for taking César as he would have done the same thing. That struck me as strange but I was glad at least that he wasn't raging.

I found out from Tomeq that Mario had called that first night to say goodnight to César, but Tomeq told him that he was already asleep. I will be forever thankful for this deception – it allowed us to escape safely. The next day Tomeq informed Mario that I had taken César.

He explained that as I had shown up he could not refuse me my child. Meanwhile, my sister Vicky had arranged for a divorce lawyer in Cape Town to be on call in case I needed legal help when we landed. We were worried that Mario would put a red flag on one of our passports to stop us at immigration.

Thankfully nothing happened and once we were safely through to the other side, I breathed a huge sigh of relief. I realised that either I hadn't seen the real Mario, or he had changed somehow and I could no longer assume the best of him.

His actions were deliberately cruel and unscrupulous. Even then, I never guessed just how far he was willing to go.

Settlement

"I'm more creative now, trying to make a birthday gift for Johan, and a costume for our holiday. I think it's helping me, it is what I enjoy doing. I have to learn to be happy with what I create and not be so critical."

LETTER FIVE

I raced to the house, anxious to be reunited with the twins.

It felt like I had been away for a long time, far too long. I hugged each one in turn, burying my face into their little necks, breathing in deeply, landing soft kisses on their cheeks. *Oh, it felt so good to hold them again!* Sadi smiled as I blew wet, noisy raspberries on their bellies, making them laugh. They looked wonderful – she had taken such good care of them and I hoped they hadn't missed me too much. Now four eyes lit up with delight as César barrelled into the room. They were all so happy to see each other.

'I can't thank you enough,' I said to Sadi, who was all packed and ready to leave. 'Thank you for staying so long. And I'm so sorry for your family. Please, go to them with my deepest condolences. Take as long as you need.'

Sadi hurried out, glad to finally be relieved of her duties so she could be with her family during their time of mourning. I had spent three weeks away from the twins and it seemed that they had changed a great deal in that time.

They were standing easier and nearly walking. We had a big pouffe in the kitchen and I watched, amazed, as they climbed up and down it, occasionally rolling off onto the floor. There were some tears but they didn't hurt themselves enough to get scared, or to stop them doing it again! *What an adventurous pair*, I marvelled.

After a few days, I met my South African divorce lawyer, Juan Smuts, a bulldog in a lovely suit. He was exactly what I needed. He seemed like a good person and I liked him immediately, but I could see that he could be tough. He worked well with my Spanish lawyer who communicated with Mario's lawyer.

Now came the long process of trying to reach an amicable divorce. I wanted my children to know their father and spend time with him. He had been a good father to César, who loved him and looked up to him. Despite everything that Mario had done, I still hoped that we could come to a quick and agreeable solution.

Over the next few months I did my best to keep up the communication, emailing Mario with frequent updates about the kids, asking him when we could Skype so that they could see him. He took days to respond. And when he did, the calls were difficult and extremely short. It was usually too late for the twins, so he mostly spoke to César. Sometimes I delayed their bedtime so they could say a quick hello, but he missed many calls, or the WiFi was too weak for a conversation. He refused to talk to me, insisting that 'talking should be left to the lawyers'. That was fine by me, but some matters I thought we should discuss directly.

One of the most pressing issues was the renewal of the kids' passports and visas. It was problematic for César as the school required a valid visa for him to be able to attend. The twins, being at kindergarten, were not a problem. But Mario would not agree to signing anything. His main excuse for not signing to renew their passports was that I would not bring them to see him. He must have realised that without valid passports I couldn't take them anywhere anyway.

I wanted him to maintain contact with the children, I always did. I told him that he could come to see the kids here anytime, but he claimed the flights were too expensive, and he believed that if he showed up to the house, I would not allow him in. Having spoken to my lawyers about the situation in Spain, they advised getting Mario to sign a paper stating that he would return the kids to me at a given date. They assured me that this would be legally binding, and we could call the police on him if he did not comply, so I told him I was quite happy for him to come to see the children in South Africa if he agreed to this.

Meanwhile, César had noticed that Mario had not been home in a long time, and, in the end, we had to tell him about the divorce on a Skype call to his dad. He seemed to take it well, though it was a relatively short call as he did not ask any questions.

I'm not sure if at five years old he had any idea what 'divorce' actually meant but as he had not seen his father much in the past two years, he was probably already used to the idea of our living separate lives. For him, nothing much would change.

Soon after my return to South Africa I 'let go' Tomeq and Agnieska as we had agreed when I saw them in Barcelona. Mario was furious when he found out and heatedly asked how I could do that to them after they had worked for us for so long. Little did he know! In the end, he rehired Tomeq to take care of the dogs and the garden though Agnieszka never returned and I often wondered what it was that made her scared to be in the same house as Mario. I knew very little of his day-to-day affairs while we were together and even less now.

I sent Mario emails with lots of pictures and updates of the kids, how they were loving swimming and spending time with Kimi, their swimming teacher. I was pleased to be able to share good news about them, that they were enjoying school and pre-school and appeared to be thriving.

Whenever I sent these emails, or when I asked for a Skype call, I always started with a polite 'Hope you are well…' And it was true. I *did* hope he was well. He was still the kids' father, after all, and I had loved him at some point. But Mario appeared stung by my attempts at civility. He said I would never have done this if I was not financially independent. I didn't know if that was true but I was very grateful for the freedom that the trust granted me.

I am aware that many women feel trapped in relationships when they are financially dependent on their partners. I was so fortunate to have an income of my own, a loving family to help me out and access to excellent legal advice. I certainly never took it for granted that I didn't rely on Mario to support me but it was a little rich for him to now find fault with that. After all, he had benefitted materially from our relationship. In my view we had both done, or not done, things that made our split inevitable. He had forged a separate life, failing to spend time with me and the children, and in the end there was very little to hold on to. The emails infuriated him.

'Don't be so fake with your greetings,' he scolded. 'I don't need your falseness when you are attacking me with your lawyers.' I think, on reflection, he didn't like the idea that I had ended our relationship. Perhaps he felt that was *his* decision to make, and his alone. That's why he didn't want to tell people – he had cultivated a certain public image and the idea that I was divorcing him contradicted that persona.

On top of that I was taking away all the benefits that being with me afforded him. Until now he had lived in a beautiful house virtually expense-free since I covered all the bills. Now that we were divorcing he would have to move out of El Palacete so we could sell it, with the money returned to the trust. None of the beneficiaries of our family trust owned any properties outright – they were all assets of the trust. Mario didn't really understand this.

He demanded a huge sum in compensation for so-called improvements to the property. I didn't see much of what he had done but I let the lawyers argue that out. It helped to know that my little email greetings annoyed him. A small and, admittedly, very petty victory. Divorce does not bring out the best in people.

Settlement

One day I was driving down from Constantia Nek towards Hout Bay to pick up César from his cooking class. I suddenly had a clear image in my mind of angel wings and a sense that everything was alright. I thought it strange as I had never felt anything like this before. It wasn't frightening or surprising either. A deep feeling of calm and assurance washed over me. I continued driving and parked at the teacher's house and walked in. When Althea, the cooking teacher, saw me she looked surprised.

'Oh, César's not here,' she said.

Here we go, I thought, *César has roped her into playing a prank on me.* I peeked around the kitchen counter, making a big pantomime of seeking him out, but Althea repeated, more seriously this time: 'No, no… it's true. César is not here.'

I realised she was serious and panicked. Had Mario flown to Cape Town, gone to the school and taken César?

Everyone knew we were getting a divorce by now, but it never occurred to me to tell the school that Mario was not allowed to take César without my prior knowledge. The calmness was suddenly gone.

Frantically, I called the school, who informed me that César was there. I breathed a sigh of relief. *Of course, Mario wouldn't come to South Africa to take César. What a stupid thought! But then again, after what had happened I can't be sure of anything anymore.* While everyone else had warned me of Mario's manipulative behaviour, I had carried around a rosy portrait of the man, always assuming the best, never for one minute suspecting him of inventing a fatal illness or being capable of holding my son hostage. I could not trust my judgement now. I told

Althea that César was in school and went to fetch him. He calmly told me that he hadn't felt like going to cooking class and decided to stay in school. His nonchalance immediately soothed me but I still told him off for not going to class!

Since we were now unable to leave the country we spent the Christmas holidays at my brother-in-law Johan's farm near Villiersdorp, about two hours west of Cape Town. It was lovely to be with Johan, Vicky and their children over Christmas, although I did miss the snow. The kids would have enjoyed sledging down hills and being dragged around by me on the frozen lake and I missed seeing my two younger sisters. Nevertheless, we made the best of it.

Mario was not happy that there was no internet connection at the Villiersdorp house. I didn't bother reminding him that he was the reason we couldn't leave the country. I had told him that he was welcome to come and see them as long as he signed a paper agreeing to return the kids at a certain time and place. But he refused.

'I should not have to sign any papers to be able to see my own children,' he fumed.

'I agree,' I said. 'But I have to insist because of what happened with César in Spain.'

I was happy for the kids to see their father. I believed that they needed to see him and I wanted them to have a good relationship, but now I was scared and traumatised by what had happened. My lawyer was adamant about Mario signing the paper.

'I don't know what you think I've done,' Mario shot back. 'It is you. *You* are making it difficult for me to see the children.'

Settlement

I sighed. *He still doesn't believe he did anything wrong!* Mario thought everyone was like him – cynical, calculating and always trying to get one up – so he frequently ascribed these motives to others. I had seen him do this to people we knew in the past but it was never directed at me before. He was unable to believe anything I said and assumed only the worst. I realised that he had always been like that, but I was disappointed that he did not seem to know me better. Or maybe he just did not want to.

The divorce dragged on for months. As we were wrangling over the details, Mario called to say we had had a break-in at El Palacete. He was still living there but had been out when the robbery took place. Now he asked me to email a list of items I had taken to South Africa so that he could make a claim on the insurance. I had no problem with that, and after I corrected some mistakes, I sent an email back to him.

From the beginning, many in my family – and my lawyers – were sceptical about this latest development. Mario claimed the robbers had taken a safe and thrown it from the second-floor window to try to smash it open. They had found his hidden stash of cash, which he could not claim on the insurance. He did not tell me the amount, but it was clear that it was enough for him to fight the insurance company for months. He didn't get anything in the end, which was strange. I think they must have smelled something fishy. Mario was furious, blaming everyone else for the difficulties he faced with the insurance claim. I heard that the guy who had insured Mario had been let go. He accused everyone from my side of getting in the way and making it impossible for him to claim the insurance. He even called a friend in South Africa and accused him of talking to the insurance company.

In August, we had a small family celebration for the twins' second birthday. We usually celebrate birthdays in the morning so that when the kids wake up, they come into a kitchen full of balloons, presents and cake with candles. César helped out by waiting with the babies in their room until I had organised everything. He was almost as excited as they were. I loved to see the amazement and delight on their faces when they toddled in to see all the gifts and giant Mickey and Minnie Mouse balloons.

César helped them to rip the wrapping off their presents and his enthusiasm and delight were infectious. We had arranged to Skype with Mario so he could see them and sing with us, which felt nice. Later in the day, we had a few of their friends from kindergarten over and it was lovely to watch the twins playing so beautifully with their friends.

While we were trying to reach an amicable solution with Mario, my lawyer Juan Smuts decided to try to hurry things along by asking a South African judge for a divorce. We could prove that we had given Mario's lawyers plenty of time to consider the settlement in the divorce papers, that communication was difficult and that I was giving him more than was necessary.

The judge saw that the agreement was more than he required and was satisfied with it. We heard from Mario's lawyers that we would get a quick response, but we never did. He had been given a month to have a lawyer appear before the judge. By this time he had a South African lawyer, but there was no reply from him either. Mario only signed the divorce agreement after his lawyer told him that the judge in South Africa would give me a divorce and he would get nothing. I later found out that his lawyers were not able to reach him for weeks on end.

He had also changed lawyers halfway through the divorce, claiming that the first ones were not doing their job. It was always such a struggle to deal with him, with all these accusations, changes in lawyers, and the inability to get anything straight out of him. The infrequent contact and erratic replies made it all so much more difficult than it needed to be.

In the end we agreed that he would be able to live in El Palacete for another year, but he needed to pay for the water, electricity and phone, which I had been doing all this time. I also agreed to pay him €300,000 which was a much reduced figure from the original sum he demanded.

I agreed to take the kids to Spain twice a year for the summer and winter holidays and pay for his flights and accommodation when he came to visit the kids in South Africa for two weeks over the Easter holiday or September break. Mario was not obligated in the settlement to contribute financially to the kids' upbringing. Instead, he would notify me when he was in a position to start contributing.

'Really? Nothing at all? Are you okay with that?' My South African lawyer was surprised when I told him this was acceptable to me.

'If it gets us to a point where we can move forward then yes,' I said. 'I'm so tired of all this. To be honest, I don't understand why he would not want to contribute. They are his children and he should feel he is helping to bring them up, but it is his choice. I won't force him. I just need to get this done and move on with my life.'

At the end of October Mario finally signed the agreement, and on November 13, 2015, a South African judge granted the divorce. A Spanish judge also had to sign it off, but the lawyers said this was a formality. Thank God it was all over! It was such a relief to finally have agreed a clear set of guidelines we could live by.

No more wrangling on the phone or email – these rules would make things so much easier. Now Mario would sign the papers for their passports and, if he broke the rules at least I had some legal recourse. I felt sad that things had become so bitter between us and knew that it would take a while for Mario to get used to this new 'us'. But now that the arrangements were settled, I hoped our relationship could move onto a better footing and that one day we might at least be able to be in the same room as each other without arguing.

In the grand schemes of things, the divorce hadn't taken that long – about a year and a half in total. I had heard nightmare stories of proceedings dragging on for three or five years and even longer in some instances. *This will help us both move forward*, I thought, *and then we can develop an amicable relationship for the sake of the kids.*

I wanted us to be able to be present at all the children's significant events in life without having to avoid each other. I wanted us to be able to hold a civil conversation someday. Now, I thought, everything would be less complicated. Looking back I can see that my optimism was entirely misplaced.

Moving Forward

"How I would have loved to see you, Octavia,
become a beautiful young girl. I keep remembering
how you, Maximo, liked to dance and sing. I am sure
that you would have done something that involves
music. I think you would be the calmest of the three.
I love you and miss you both so."

It happened at the airport, just before we were about to fly to
Spain for Christmas. With the divorce settled, Mario signed
the authorisations to have the children's passports renewed
and I booked plane tickets. The children were due to spend
two weeks with Mario and he had agreed that their Spanish
teacher Marga would stay with him to help him out. That
was a comfort to me as it had been a long time since the
twins and César had seen their father and it would take them
a while to get used to being with him, especially in a new
place. I had packed everyone's clothes the day before, my
chest feeling a little tight, my breathing not always steady
but I assumed this was because of all the crazy last minute
arrangements. There was just so much to do in a short space

81

of time. But just after we cleared immigration, it hit me full force. I couldn't get a full breath inside me.

Shit, what's happening?

I started gulping in air like a fish out of water. Marga looked over at me in alarm. No matter how much I tried to force the air into my lungs I didn't feel like I was getting enough breath. My shoulders rose up and down, I put a hand on my chest but it felt so restricted.

'Julia? Are you okay?'

'Can't… seem… to… ugh… catch… my… breath,' I panted.

'Come over here,' she pulled me to one side of the corridor. 'I think you're having a panic attack. Just stop for a second here and take a minute.'

We walked to the side of the corridor and now I realised she was right. This was anxiety. My chest still heaved up and down as I sucked in short, shallow breaths but just knowing what it was helped me to calm down a little. At the end of this flight I would have to say goodbye to the children for two weeks. Amid all the preparations for the journey I hadn't let myself think about it. Now I allowed myself to admit that I felt frightened. The last time I had left my child with Mario he had refused to give him back. Thank God Marga was here with me! If she hadn't realised what was happening it could have been so much worse. As it was, it was horrible not to be able to take a full breath of air.

During the flight, I tried to reassure myself that we had put in place sensible arrangements to ensure a smooth transition of care. I would leave César with Mario on the day of arrival and then he would take the twins every day from 10am till 5pm every day for three days so that they could get used to him before they stayed the night. Marga would help Mario take care of the kids and be a familiar face for them to make their stay easier. If anything happened she knew what to do and who to call.

The babies were still only two and a half so they needed a lot of care. Crucially, Marga was Spanish so she could communicate with Mario. I had chosen her specifically so that she could continue to talk to the children in Spanish. I already spoke to them in German and the general rule was that one should not mix languages when children were learning how to talk, but I did not want them to lose that part of their heritage that came from their father's side. My mother, sisters and I also had roots in Spain.

At El Palacete, Mario took a long time to open the gate and let us in. The kids were hungry and tired from such a long trip. They were also a bit apprehensive to see their father. While César was excited, Octavia didn't say much, and Maximo kept saying that he did not want to stay with his father.

Once inside the house, César ran into his father's arms while Octavia slowly walked over to give him a hug. Maximo held onto my leg for a while but he also went to say hello to his father after he saw his siblings reacting so positively to Mario. I went into the kitchen but there was hardly anything to eat.

Mario complained that no one had told him what he needed to have in the house for the kids. I was surprised as

I had sent a list of foods to my lawyer but now I gave him the list again. It wasn't rocket science – he could have just bought a few essentials like fruit, cookies, pasta, cheese, ham, bread and milk. After about half an hour we left César with Mario and headed to Ana's flat.

By the time we arrived at 5pm, the twins were fast asleep. It had been such a long day I was grateful that my sister had thoughtfully prepared dinner in advance so now we woke Maximus and Octavia up to feed them. While they were eating, the doorbell rang. Ana looked surprised.

'No one usually calls at this time,' she frowned as she went to answer the intercom.

It was Mario. He said angrily that César didn't want to stay with him. It was a bit difficult to understand him though as César was crying in the background. Ana buzzed them in and I went downstairs to see them. When we opened the door César ran into my arms.

'I want to stay here with you and the twins,' he wept, clutching my waist. I was surprised to see my son in such a state and behind him Mario, his face like thunder.

'He wants to stay here,' he said through gritted teeth.

I tried to explain that that was hard on César, that maybe he also needed a slow introduction to his father again after not seeing him since October the previous year. But Mario didn't want to hear it and left in a foul mood.

I prepared dinner for César who calmed down quickly. After a quarter of an hour, the doorbell rang, it was Mario again. This time *he* was crying. He felt bad for César, he said, and wanted to give him a kiss and a hug. César got up from the table for a quick hug but he was keen to return to his dinner.

'He just needs time,' I said to Mario after he was out of earshot. 'This is hard on him as well. He hasn't seen you in a long time and he's used to being with the twins. So let's make it easier for him. Why don't we do the 10-5 routine with all three kids? Then you can have them full time from December 15 to the 26.'

Mario nodded sorrowfully and for the first time in a long time I felt I was seeing his true emotions, not just a blank, thousand-mile stare.

'Yeah, okay,' he agreed. 'If it's best for César. Tell him I'll see him tomorrow.'

I closed the door and that night the children all settled down quite nicely, the twins sleeping on mattresses on the floor in my room and César in his cousin's room. It helped that they were exhausted from the long trip.

After the rocky start, the days went well. The kids left happily with Mario on the next few mornings. I didn't have to worry about anything, mainly because Marga was there to help Mario. It gave me such peace of mind, I was able to relax. Mario had never taken care of small children on his own before. Even when César was little, he was not that involved. He became much more so once more interaction was possible. But with such little childcare experience, it felt like a very big ask to make him responsible for three children at once.

In the meantime, I took a meeting with my lawyer. There was nothing significant to discuss, so it was over quite quickly, but she informed me that she had not sent the shopping list to Mario.

'He's always complaining that he's not able to be a father,' she explained. 'I thought he should have the full experience and figure it out for himself.'

I found it quite funny that she took the initiative to do that, although I doubt that Mario would have seen it the same way.

On Tuesday, I had prepared all the children's things, ready to pack in Mario's car for their long stay. It seemed like he had hired a car and driver as I didn't recognise either. I later found out that Mario's lawyer had lent him a car and driver. I found that somewhat strange but didn't worry about it. There were so many things Mario did that didn't make sense to me.

The kids had to lift their legs to make room, which neither Maximo nor César liked, so they left screaming but I assumed that all would be well once they got going. Marga sent me a message a little later saying that Mario wanted the passports. Without thinking I agreed. Although I was hesitant, I didn't know how I could say no and called Vicky for advice.

'No way!' she exclaimed. 'It's out of the question. You shouldn't give them to him.'

My lawyer agreed.

'I suggest you tell him that I have possession of the passports right now and if there is an emergency, he can collect them from me.'

Naturally, Mario didn't like this and said he didn't need an emergency; he was entitled to have them. I suggested we let the lawyers sort it out.

Moving Forward

'I will speak to my lawyer and we'll get the judge to force you to hand the passports over,' he fumed.

'Okay,' I said, trying not to rise to his provocations.

'And by the way, I'm giving Marga the day off on Wednesday,' he went on. 'I'm taking the children to see my parents, and I want the visit to be relaxed with no strangers present.'

'Things will probably be calmer with Marga's help.'

'Nonsense. She's not needed. Tell her.'

So I told Marga and she also tried to convince him that she could be a help to him but was unsuccessful. He told her he would sleep at his parents' place for one or two nights, and that she should prepare an overnight bag for the kids.

The next morning Marga told me that he was on his way to a judge. *Oh God, what now?* I sent a message to my lawyer about this development and a little while later she called to let me know Mario had spoken to his own lawyer who had told him to stop being difficult, that he didn't need the passports and to turn around.

Thankfully, he listened. Mario then left Marga in Cornella, a town just outside Barcelona where her family lived, and took the kids to visit his parents. The children seemed quite happy and did not cry when they saw me on Skype later that day. They also seemed to be delighted to be with him which mitigated my anxiety somewhat.

I had dinner with Alicia, a mutual friend of Mario with whom I had kept in touch. Even though there was a big age gap we always got along very well. She was a strong woman who had divorced her husband young, when everyone she knew, including her family, was against it. She was a working single mother, an estate agent, who did not shrink away from difficulties and I appreciated her straight-talking attitude. She also knew a great deal more than I about Mario's shady financial dealings.

'Mario can't have a bank account as the Spanish tax authority have him in their sights for evading taxes,' she explained. 'The minute he puts anything in his name the government will take it.'

That explained why all his business dealings and the cars he 'owned' were all under other people's names. That also explained why he had been making it hard for me to pay him the agreed-upon settlement. He wanted to use his associate Daniel's bank account to receive the divorce money I agreed to pay him, but my lawyers vehemently refused, insisting we send the money either to his account or the lawyer's. Alicia further found out that Mario had put El Palacete up for sale through a tiny agency who had called her offering to sell her 'the best house in Barcelona'.

The cheek of it! El Palacete wasn't his property to sell but I imagined he did this so that he could claim a commission or to muddy the waters, making the sale of the house more complicated. It wasn't clear. He had put the property on for a lower price. *What did it mean? Does he do these things deliberately to make me anxious?* My lawyer certainly seemed to think so.

'He knows how to press your buttons, Julia,' she said when I spoke to her. 'You've got to try not to let him get to you.'

The next morning Marga called to tell me that Mario wanted to talk to me, but not directly, it had to be through her. I rolled my eyes skywards. *How can a grown man be so petty and childish?*

'Okay,' I said. 'Go ahead.'

Marga then repeated his words: 'I don't want Marga here. I don't want someone looking over my shoulder all the time. Nor do I feel safe leaving her in the house while I'm out as she could go through my papers. I will not pay for her food or let her sleep on a bed at night.'

I was incredulous. We had agreed that he would accept Marga. It was in the divorce papers. He thought she was my spy when in fact she was only there to help him manage. Marga then whispered to me: 'It's fine. I can get my own food and sleep on the floor.'

'No, I can't let you do that,' I replied.

I thought hard about what to do. If I went round there to pick the children up, Mario would resist, we'd cause a scene and make the children feel unsafe. I didn't want that.

'Do you think he can look after the children on his own?' I asked Marga.

'Yes, I think he can. The kids are happy with him and having fun.'

The few times I had talked to them they seemed fine and content. This was the most important thing for me. She could not stay there under those conditions, and the kids would have noticed something was wrong.

'Okay, you can leave,' I told her. 'Get a taxi. Go and spend some time with your family.'

From now on Mario was on his own. I just hoped he was up to the job.

St. Moritz

*"Some days are hard, and others I can talk about you
or about what happened and be quite alright with it."*

LETTER NINE

I walked along the peaceful streets of St. Moritz, the houses
lit by twinkling Christmas lights on either side, snow crunch-
ing underfoot and laying picturesquely across the rooftops.
It was so beautiful here, I thought, nestled in the mountains.
We usually came to St. Moritz every winter, and with all the
snow, it always looked magical.

I had driven here with Ana on December 18 for the
holidays and now I really wanted to relax and enjoy myself
but it wasn't that easy to disconnect my mind from the
children. Whatever I was doing, my mind was always with
them. *What are they doing? Are they okay?* I was their primary
carer, the person who was normally with them every hour of
every day, so it was hard suddenly having no contact at all. I
couldn't let go. *Is this normal?* I wondered. *Is it just me?* I didn't
know if I was just missing them in the usual way or whether
I had control issues.

I emailed Mario, asking if we could arrange a time I could

see them on Skype. He always agreed, but when I called he didn't answer or found an excuse. He told me that the twins were asleep, when it wasn't their nap time, or that César was playing with a friend.

I usually asked well in advance to give them plenty of time to make a plan but this didn't seem to register. One day he wrote: 'It would be convenient if you could let me know beforehand.' The next day he sent a message: 'We are at a fair, the babies are in bed. We will try again tomorrow.' I freaked out a bit and asked him who was looking after the kids if he and César were at a fair.

He replied later, clearly annoyed:

'Read the message correctly. Don't get anxious, don't interrogate me and don't question my attitude to taking care of the babies. The kids are fine. All three are always with me. I don't think it's necessary that I have to justify myself to a person who is always surrounded by domestic help. I don't ask you with whom you left them. I think that common sense and my love for my kids is beyond question. It doesn't help me to receive calls from an unknown number when I am not attentive of the mobile because I am looking after the kids. You have practically talked to them every day, something that I can't say when you have them. And I am not an expert in child pedagogy, like your lawyer, who once dared to suggest I should call the kids on particular days and hours of the week. I have on my side people who are sensible, thorough and kind, who suggest what is best for the kids and their parents. And I agree with them. You can't also pretend that I should be dependent on your calls from an unknown number every minute. Julia, sincerely, I want the best for our kids, and that, most importantly, they are loved and see their mother and father. Tomorrow I will be at my brother's house. When we are finished eating, we will Skype.'

That made me feel terrible. Was I being overprotective and anxious? Perhaps, but it wasn't fair to agree to Skype and then fail to pick up. I worried that he was telling the kids that I was not calling them.

There were so many things I wanted to say to him after that email, but I thought it best to leave it. I wanted to know, for example, why my number was unknown to him. And what did he mean – 'surrounded by help'? What are the suggestions he is getting? Why doesn't he tell me so we can discuss them? I had no idea who was helping him with the kids. He knew Sadi and Marga well. I didn't need to know what they got up to when they were with him. It was all just very difficult and I struggled to contain my own feelings of frustration and worry.

But I knew I would not get anywhere with him. The only thing that mattered was that our kids were happy. I had to learn to accept the limited amount of information and time I could see them when they were with Mario, but I had not realised how hard it was going to be.

This was their first time with their father on their own in over a year and I was nervous. I could also understand his point of view that it was difficult to be apart from the kids. But we had spent two years before our divorce living apart, with him leaving the kids with me. He was surely used to it. Of course I knew it was different now that we were officially divorced but why make everything so difficult? We weren't able to communicate effectively.

It was true that my lawyer had suggested a routine for Mario to talk to the kids over the phone. She felt it would be easier for them, something more reliable. But anything that my lawyer suggested was out of the question for him. As it stood, the kids had very erratic contact with Mario, mostly because he never showed up for calls when I suggested them or would miss the ones that he had arranged.

I later found out, through the kids, that he had a nanny to help him, which I had nothing against, but then why not just tell me this and put my mind at rest? He said he wanted me to stop worrying but it felt like everything was done to make the separation harder.

Mario finally called me on Skype from his brother's house. The twins sounded good and didn't cry when they saw me. César had no real interest in talking to me, which was also a good sign. But it was a pity that his video didn't work, so I was not able to see the children. Mario then sent an email saying that the kids had had a great time and played all day. He noted that the connection with me wasn't good and that he would try to call the next day so I could talk to them.

I wrote back saying that I would be more than happy to speak to them if they wanted to, but as they sounded well, it wasn't necessary. I didn't want to force the kids to speak to me. Hearing from them that they were happy was all I needed. A few pictures would have been great, but the request landed on deaf ears. I was grateful for the email he had sent. It seemed that he had maybe understood how hard this was for me. It appeared he was showing some empathy.

After lunch the next day I returned to the house, to see that he had called. I tried to call back, but he was no longer connected. I thought it strange as we had not agreed to a call. I emailed him to say that I was back and available, keeping the iPad open, hoping he would call, but I did not hold my breath. I had to accept that even though I doubted that he would be able to do this on his own, he seemed to be managing.

Two days later I sent Mario an email in the morning asking if I could call his mobile to talk to the kids, or to contact me from the home phone, as I was still paying the bill. I thought maybe he wanted to save on costs for some reason. I didn't want him to use that as an excuse. I only wanted to hear their voices. He replied:

'Strangely, you are worried now about these small domestic expenses when you have not paid your debt for more than 15 months, the same amount of time that I have not seen my kids. Of course, you are worried because it is convenient for you. Always egocentric. Now that your psychologist lawyers tell me that's what I am, I will tell you. What I want is that the children are happy and with you, I do not want any more contact than is necessary because of our children. Underneath your constant lies and hypocrisies exist a bad person from whom I do not want to know anything. It's very easy 'Hello Mario and Kind regards' when you and your lawyers have made me suffer so. Avoid regards and fake wishes. I only want short and to the point messages with you. I have no problem in paying for anything for the children and as you can tell I also want them to see their mother. Today we are going to the circus. If you don't believe me, ask your detectives.'

I replied: 'Dear Mario, Will there be no moment during the day when I could talk to the kids for two minutes? Kind regards, Julia'

He was excellent in pulling me every which way. In his previous email, he seemed more open and more communicative, but he quickly changed his tune. My anxiety did not help in these situations. It always seemed to take me to a place of doubt. I did not hear back from him, but I heard from my lawyer. His lawyer had not been able to make contact, and his last email to her was to say that he wanted the cheque to be made out to a third person, which he already knew we would not do.

This was the cheque that he claimed I had not paid in 15 months. I had been trying, but he made it impossible. If there was no contact with Mario, the cheque would be made out to his lawyer, as we had discussed, which would have to be signed in front of a notary. He would then have a month to collect it. I told my lawyer about Mario's email and what had happened, and she sighed.

'Oh Julia, he has so much hate towards you, your family and even us lawyers, he just lashes out whenever he can.'

He had still not signed the form for me to travel with the children in Europe, but I wasn't worried about that.

It was hard to be without the children over Christmas. My first alone. I tried to speak to them but the internet was down. Instead, I watched my nieces and nephews enjoying the snow, the lights, the beautifully decorated Christmas tree, the smell of baking cookies and the presents. And all I could think about was my children.

We had arranged for me to collect the children from Spain so they could come to Switzerland with me for a few days but Mario kept changing the arrangements. It made me nervous. Would Mario bring them to the airport? Would there be a problem with papers? Would they be late? What would be missing? Most importantly, would they be happy? All I wanted was to be with them and wrap them up in my arms.

I woke at 3.30am on the day of the handover, after not having slept much, just thinking about all the things that could go wrong. As it turned out the transfer was a complete mess. I flew to Barcelona then went to the house just in time so see him driving down the road but I could not see if the kids were in the car. Now I wasn't sure what to do. *Should I continue or turn back? And why was he driving like that?* At the house it was quiet and there seemed to be no one around.

All I could hear were the dogs barking inside. Marga arrived, and we left for the airport with the taxi that she came in. I was worried that he would do something stupid, like last time. We were both anxious and discussed the last week in detail. At the airport, we waited until the appointed time, but were in the wrong place. Mario wanted to meet at the consulate parking, but the instructions he had given me were incorrect. When I got there, he was with the kids and their luggage. They were delighted to see me and I was thrilled to be reunited with them. They all seemed a little dirty, but happy, and they were with me, which was all that mattered. Although César looked a bit sad to be parting from his father, I took that as a good sign.

The plane ride wasn't too bad. I was just relieved that they were fine and seem to have enjoyed the time with their father. When we arrived in St. Moritz they opened their presents. It took them a while to fall asleep that night after what must have seemed like a very eventful day.

The next day, Sunday, César went off to skiing school, while I took the twins to the supermarket and then to the lake. They spoke with their father for a bit and were happy. But they didn't nap in the day and had many difficult nights. Octavia screamed for me to come and hug and kiss her various times during the night. It was the first time they had really experienced snow and they loved playing in it and being pulled by the sled. But they were a bit unsure about walking on it as it was quite icy. They fell a lot and were not the happiest when they got hurt. But it was understandable, they were experiencing so many changes it must have been confusing for them.

Some time during these days in St. Moritz, I sent an email to Mario telling him that César wanted to talk to him and asking him how we should organise the pick-ups and drop-offs for the 2nd and 8th of January. He replied that we would do what we had agreed to in our divorce papers. This meant I would drop them off at the house and Marga would stay too, as agreed in our settlement. Then, on the 8th he would drop them off at Ana's flat. I didn't hear back from him so I assumed the arrangements were acceptable.

Precious Scars

He did, however, email Josep, and as always copied me in, to say that his lawyer had recommended he go ahead and report me for fiscal fraud in Spain. Josep was on holiday and did not reply. Mario sent me another email saying at least Josep would benefit from this because he would be working for us in this matter and would earn wages. Mario had been using this for a while as a threat. My lawyers told me to ignore him because he did not have a leg to stand on. Alicia had already told me that he was on the radar for fiscal irregularities, so it was doubtful that he would do anything. I knew these were empty threats. Even so, I was nervous. Maybe that was his aim, to have me constantly on edge.

On our last day in St. Moritz we had the first family lunch of the year at El Paradiso. We headed up the mountain in the ski lift. Everything went well until Octavia made a move to get closer to the edge of the ski lift so she could see down. I had to hold onto both of them to prevent them from slipping through the gap. Octavia didn't like that one bit. After a lot of screaming and squirming around, she lost both her shoes, which made her scream more.

Once we got to the restaurant I stayed outside with Octavia trying to calm her down. My father went down to get the shoes where they had fallen at the steepest part of the slope. I let her cry it out as I was unable to do anything else. By the time she had calmed down our food was waiting for us on the table. The twins did not want to leave my side, but after a while they saw the fun that César was having in the snow and joined him. It was nice to see them relaxed. Whatever was going on in their little heads seemed to have passed for now. They were obviously suffering from the changes and it must have been difficult for them not fully understanding what was suddenly happening.

The next day we left early in the taxi for Zurich to take our flight to Barcelona. As I collected the luggage from the carousel I saw I had a message from Tomeq. On the way to the house I called him. He said Mario was trying to get Marga out of the house by any means necessary. He had taken the bedsheets off the bed and planned to ask her to go out to buy some food, and not let her back into the house. I realised it would be a losing battle to try to have Marga stay with him.

Mario took his time to answer the door again. While I was getting the luggage into the property, he told Marga that he had replied to her earlier message saying that he didn't need her. I told him that Marga would stay, as stipulated in the papers that Mario had signed. Ignoring me, he then told Marga: 'Ask your employer for money as I will not pay for taxis, food or anything else.'

'In the agreement it stipulates that you have to take care of her,' I said. But I knew it was useless to argue so I let it drop and gave her €300. The taxi driver then drove me to Ana's place. By now I felt so frustrated and upset I vented at the taxi driver. He told me he had also been through a difficult divorce and was understanding of my situation. It felt good to hear from someone who had been through something similar. I didn't know anyone else who had experienced anything like this.

At Ana's place, I unpacked, opened a beer, and started to update my diary. I'd started writing a diary after everything that happened with César. Things felt so unreal I felt I had to write it all down to record what happened and to try to process how I felt. I didn't want to react in the moment but get a handle on how everything was unfolding. As I was writing, I got a message from Marga asking me to call her. My heart rate shot up in an instant. My first thoughts were with the children – were they alright?

'Mario wants me to give you a message,' she said when we spoke. 'He's telling me that he wants you to know that I am *persona non grata* in his house.'

Mario had made it impossible for her to stay so I told her that I understood this was a bad situation for her and that she should leave. The kids had been fine before and would be again. Later that night Marga called me from the car on her way home.

'The babies are fine,' she assured me. 'Though César wanted me to stay. I told him I would love to but his father didn't want me to remain as he wanted to take care of the kids on his own. Then César said to his father: "But Papa, when the babies cry a lot in the morning Marga could help you look after them because you are so tired and get angry."'

'Oh dear, he would not have liked that.'

'No, but he didn't say anything to César.'

'It's fine. I'm sure it will be fine.'

At Ana's I tried to relax but it felt as if I was just marking time. In my diary I wrote:

'I've been running and walking and right now I am in a bar called Eclipse enjoying a Moscow Mule. There are not many people here, but at least I am not in front of the TV

stuffing my face with chocolate, like the last two nights. Am I feeling sorry for myself? I think to some extent yes, but I am not sure why. I know this is good for me, and I also need to enjoy the time off. There are no tantrums, spilled water, wasted food, dirty nappies and endless cleaning up. Just me time.

By always expecting the worst of Mario, will I not get the worst from him? I somehow have to change my mindset and become more optimistic about him, or of the situation and the future. My negativity will also affect the kids, which I do not want. I think there is a possibility of being surprised at what Mario is capable of as a father. I have to give him a chance and accept that the next few years will be difficult until he has gotten over the resentment and anger towards my family and me. I sometimes find myself daydreaming that he has a girlfriend who softens his anger towards me a bit, that he relaxes and has another child with her and sees that it would be better to try and make the best of a bad situation.

Over time it will be better and more comfortable for everyone. I will get used to it. Importantly, the kids have this time with their father. I think I will also enjoy it when Mario comes to South Africa, as I will be home. It's different when you are alone in a place not your own. Let's see if he does come. I hope so, as César will enjoy it. He keeps saying he wants to show his father all the places he goes to, mainly his school, the waterpark in Muizenberg and the beach. This situation is still new, and hopefully, in time I won't talk about my divorce when I write, but about other things.'

Iiro

"I had already noticed a change in both of you after you turned three. You were more understanding, able to accept things. Maybe it was just me, but it seemed to have gotten easier. Now I will never know what you would have turned out to be like."

LETTER TWELVE

The children's eyes lit up in wonder as the tall, blond man ran a coin over his knuckles. It sparkled tantalisingly as it moved swiftly across his hand – then disappeared altogether. The next minute he plucked it from behind a little girl's head and they all erupted in a collective: 'Whoah!'

I laughed at their reaction, noting that César was among the gaggle of wide-eyed kids, his face a picture of astonishment. I recognised the man entertaining them but couldn't quite recall his name.

'Remind me, who is your friend doing magic for the children?' I asked my sister Vicky.

'Oh that's Iiro Seppänen,' she said. 'You've met him before, I think.'

'Yes, I have.' Now I recalled a time several years before at another birthday party. Back then he had a girlfriend but I hadn't noticed him with anyone on this trip.

'Is he with anyone?' I asked.

'Not as far as I know. Single. No kids.'

'No kids?' I replied. Now it was my turn for astonishment. 'You're joking? Look! He's fantastic with children.'

The group once again laughed with delight at Iiro's impromptu close-up magic show. For a man without children of his own he was certainly great with everyone else's.

We were in Morocco to celebrate Vicky's 40th birthday with a few of her close friends. There was a whole week of activities planned and since we were travelling to the desert and sleeping in tents I decided it would be too much for the twins. So while César and I flew out at the end of January, I left Octavia and Maximo with Sadi. She adored the twins and was great with them so I didn't have any qualms about leaving them in her care.

I loved being in Marrakesh. Aside from the beautiful surroundings, it was great to spend a little quality time with César – he was a devoted big brother but there was no question the twins took up a lot of my time and attention. At the same time I enjoyed being in adult company. But more than anything, I found myself attracted to someone for the first time in years. It came as quite a shock but there was definitely a spark between me and Iiro.

We spoke quite a lot over the next week and I found out that he had started his career as a magician but was now one of the founders of the World Wingsuit League. I'd heard of wingsuit flying before though I'd never met anyone who actually did it. What an extraordinary sport! Iiro was now retired from flying himself but he organised various events around the world. The whole week I followed him around like a besotted teenager.

On our last night we had dinner with a friend of Vicky's, then went back to the hotel where we had a couple of drinks. In all this time he had never made any kind of move so as we walked back to our respective rooms, I decided there was nothing to lose and I would kiss him. Thankfully, when we said goodbye, we both went in for the kiss.

Iiro had to leave early the next day but on his way to the airport he started following me on Facebook and we started communicating through Messenger. As fate would have it, he was shortly due to visit friends in South Africa so we arranged to see each other then.

Two weeks later Iiro was in Cape Town and we met for lunch a couple of times before I invited him back to the house to meet the twins. He arrived with balloon animals and some simple magic tricks the twins could understand. They had not seen magic performed before and were in awe.

Of course, they adored him. And César was very excited to see him again as they had gotten along well on our trip to Morocco. Iiro spent the last two nights of his trip staying at our house and by the time he left we had become really close. It was exciting to be in a new relationship and held the promise of a happier future after several difficult years.

Meanwhile, everything with Mario went badly as usual. I was frustrated by the inconsistent contact with the kids as well as his angry and frequent changes of plan. The only thing I could rely on with Mario was his unreliability. He planned to come to South Africa for the Easter holidays, he said, so I booked the flight and rented an apartment for him near the beach in Hout Bay where I thought the kids would have fun. He asked me to send the booking information on two or three occasions, and each time I did.

It seemed to me that he did not believe me, or he had forgotten. He also changed his mind a couple of times as to whether he was coming or not. He said that his father was very ill, and he didn't want to leave the country in case something happened. Then a few days before he was due to fly, he talked to César and told him he was coming. I was so happy for my son, who was thrilled at the thought of being with his father again.

But on the day he was due to fly I didn't get a message confirming he was on his way. I contacted Tomeq to ask if he had taken Mario to the airport and he replied that he had not. I asked my travel agent to check if he had checked in. He hadn't. I was disappointed again. Why did it keep surprising me? César was heartbroken. I hardly knew what to say to him anymore and struggled to hide my own frustration. Why hadn't he said anything? It was unfair to raise our son's hopes like that and simply fail to turn up.

Mario called a couple of days later to say that his father was sick, and he did not want to risk travelling. It was understandable, of course, but why wait to tell us? And why had he avoided telling César and the twins himself? He had saddled me with the responsibility of handling their disappointment caused by his actions.

I tried not to let it get to me. Instead, I focussed on the children and putting a little time into my own goals. A friend had mentioned the previous year that he was going to do a half Ironman in France in May. He suggested that I do it too. My immediate reaction had been: 'No! Are you crazy?'. A half Ironman consists of a 1.9km swim, a 90km bicycle ride and a 21km marathon. But the seed had been planted.

Since I was already in the gym four or five times a week doing weights and interval training, I thought that there was no harm in training when the kids were in school. And if I didn't take part, for whatever reason, I would still reap the benefits of getting fit. The first thing I needed was a decent racing bike so I went to the bike shop. When I mentioned the half Ironman the owner suggested I join their cycling group.

'We go out every morning at 5.30am and cycle all round Constantia, up Chapman's Peak and around the coast,' she explained. 'You should come along, see how you like it. It would definitely help with your training.' Reluctantly, and with some trepidation, I agreed.

At 5.30am the next morning we met up not far from my house. I was pleased to see the female shop owner here too – one other woman among a sea of men. Fit men, as it turned out. Once we were all assembled we set off and within the first few minutes, they were gone, cycling much faster than I could. *God, I'll never keep up!* I thought as I peddled up and down the wide roads. We cycled uphill – the main group stopping every now and then to allow me to catch up – before taking a roundabout and then heading down the mountain into Hout Bay.

Chapman's Peak was a very windy road and incredibly scenic with the mountain on one side and the ocean on the other. But I was freaked out by the speed the other riders were going. They flew down at an incredible pace, trying to gain as much momentum as possible. I hurtled down the mountain at what felt like a terrific speed myself, though I had my brakes on the whole time, petrified of taking a bend too fast and flying off the side of the mountain, or colliding with oncoming traffic. *At least there aren't many cars on the road at this time of the day*, I thought, as I took on one blind bend after another.

At the bottom I saw that all the riders had stopped at a set of traffic lights so I let myself go a little faster to catch up. At the lights I put the brakes on to come to a stop, realising too late that my feet were still clipped into the pedals. I wobbled a little. Then, unable to stop myself, I fell sideways. There were cars in front and behind me, and it must have looked so funny. If I had seen it from behind I would have burst out laughing too. *Next time, don't forget to clip off your shoes, dummy!*

At the end of the ride, I felt exhausted but exhilarated and resolved to join them again the next week. It surprised me that I enjoyed the cycling so much. We met once a week on weekdays and then every second Saturday for a longer cycle lasting over two hours. I looked forward to these early morning rides when the sun rose up over the ocean and we'd see dolphins frolicking in the bays and sometimes whales breaching in the distance. Maybe the cycling also helped me get rid of the tension and subconscious anger and stress I was holding onto.

It felt good and I loved being outside in the early mornings. On the weekends we did longer rides either into town and back through Camps Bay or from Constantia to Simon's Town, over the hills to the other side. So when the time came I decided to go ahead with the race because I had put in so much time and effort.

In May I flew to Aix-en-Provence for the competition and was thrilled when Iiro said he would meet me there for moral support. Unfortunately the swimming was cancelled due to the cold, so we went straight onto the bikes. It was lovely scenery but cycling for a fast time wasn't as enjoyable as cycling for leisure.

The running was more fun as people lined the streets to cheer us on. In the sea of friendly faces there was only one I recognised, that was Iiro's, as he bobbed and weaved in and out of the crowds, trying to take pictures of me. I finished in 3 hours 14 minutes for the cycling and 2 hours 3 minutes for the run which really wasn't too bad. Iiro cheered me all the way. He was so supportive and seemed genuinely interested in what I was doing. That felt really nice. Mario had never shown any interest in me or my activities. If anything, I felt he resented anything that might draw my attention away from him. It was a welcome change to feel encouraged by my partner.

At the end of it all, I was exhausted and headed back to the hotel for a warm bath and early dinner as I had an early start for the long flight back home to the kids the next day. It had been an intense challenge but worth it and I was proud of myself for going through with it. I had gone some way to building up my self-esteem again after the bruising divorce.

For the summer holidays I decided that Mario would probably make another fuss about the nanny, so I flew to Spain without her. He had managed before without any help and I didn't want to create unnecessary problems. This time I dropped them all off at El Palacete and although Maximo was not pleased, César and Octavia were quite happy. At least they have each other, I consoled myself as I drove away that day. It always was so hard to leave them but I knew I had to let go and allow their father to take care of them. Thankfully, Tomeq sent me pictures of the kids having fun and enjoying themselves. I could see they were well and this reassured me greatly. It meant I wasn't so desperate to speak to them as often.

I knew I would need something to do while the children were with Mario so instead of just hanging around Barcelona, I made plans with Iiro. I flew to Los Angeles, where he was working, and we took a sightseeing and wine tasting tour together. It was fantastic and we got really close during this time, though I couldn't help feeling guilty for spending so much time away from the kids.

After two weeks we flew back to Europe together, stopping off in Helsinki to meet Iiro's parents and some of his friends. I tried to learn a few words in Finnish but it was tricky. Iiro and I always spoke in English as Finnish was not an easy language to learn and though I spoke three languages – English, German and Spanish – I had learned these as a child. I didn't consider myself a particularly instinctive linguist.

'Don't worry,' Iiro laughed. 'Finnish isn't close to anything, apart from Estonian. In the tree of language development there are all these different roots that make languages similar. And then, over here, there is a tiny little bush, and that is Finnish and Estonian!'

Finally, after their holiday with their father, I picked up the children. I was unsure how Mario would react to seeing him so Iiro did not come in. César was sad to say goodbye to his father, but he perked up a little when he saw Iiro. We all went on to Palamos together as I planned to introduce him to the rest of my family. There we enjoyed a week's beach holiday with the rest of my family.

The children spent most of the time naked, running around and splashing in the water, sitting on me and eating ice cream. We took a boat trip which the twins only liked once we stopped to swim. The coast of Palamos is full of idyllic little coves, with small beaches and calm waters. It was beautiful. My parents were welcoming to Iiro and seemed pleased that I had found happiness again. We returned to South Africa in the first week of July and I felt that overall it had been a very successful holiday. The children had had a good time with their father and I had managed to enjoy myself too. Things were definitely improving.

Now the time was fast approaching for Mario to move out of El Palacete. He had lived there for a year without paying rent or a single bill so in October 2016 I sent him an email reminding him that by mid-November he had to be out and asking how he wanted to arrange the handover of the keys.

He replied that he had moved out a month ago. I was surprised and contacted my lawyers. I could understand that he had not told me, but why had his lawyer not said anything? Perhaps they didn't know either. He didn't even bother giving me the keys. I would have changed the locks anyway, but what was the sense in doing things the hard way? I was trying to be amicable and understanding but he always made things so difficult.

Mario had been paying Tomeq to see that the house was more or less in order so I asked him to meet my lawyers at the property so that they could take stock of the situation. They arrived to find that house had been completely emptied.

Mario had taken all the art and furniture that I had left behind. He had even taken doors specially made for the dressing room and painted with hunting motifs. If he ever used them, he would have to make cupboards specifically for those doors!

I didn't even have proof that the items he took were mine because the receipts were in a folder in the desk that he had also taken. I could have screamed! There were some things there that I loved, things I had bought with my own money before I even met Mario. But I hadn't taken them to South Africa because he'd insisted he didn't want the place to be empty while he was still living there. I had agreed, never imagining we would split and one day and he would take everything with him.

It was so vindictive, so childish. It was also depressing and a little sad. I could not see how I was going to be able to get anything back. He could just claim the items had been stolen in the robbery. In the end, I decided there was nothing I could do so I let it all go. If he was trying to control me by upsetting me I would not let him succeed.

Besides, I was in love. I was sure Iiro was too, though we hadn't said it to each other yet. Whenever he texted, he started off saying, "My love". He sent me a picture from Rio of a heart in the sand with an arrow through it and our names next to it. It was so sweet! His work took him all over the world but he was brilliant at staying in touch and we met whenever it was possible.

In October I received the sad news that my grandfather had died and flew to Switzerland for the funeral. He had been fighting cancer for a while but had beaten it and for a while his health was more or less fine. It came as a shock to me that he had passed away so suddenly.

With the divorce over, Mario and I settled into a routine of sorts. He talked to the kids more frequently at the arranged times. He still refused to speak to me but I hoped this too would change with time. For the Christmas holidays I decided the kids should spend the entire three weeks with Mario as going back and forth didn't make things any easier for them or me. Mario came to fetch them at the airport. As he had moved out of El Palacete, he took them to his new house, or so I assumed, because he would not tell me. This had been an ongoing discussion with no resolution.

When I talked about it with my lawyers they suggested hiring the same detective as before to find out where the kids were going to stay. I agreed, thinking I should at least know where they were. The detective followed them to a house in a small village outside Girona, which Mario appeared to be renting. It was infuriating to have to go to such lengths but Mario left me with little choice. His actions were deliberately spiteful and showed he had no interest in building a good relationship of mutual trust and respect for the sake of the children. Instead he did everything possible to build a wall between us.

I had to remind myself that he had never been forthcoming about his whereabouts, even with his own parents. He was quite secretive with them, lying about our plans to avoid having to see them. Perhaps this evasiveness was part of his nature.

It was hard to be without the kids again at Christmas. It felt strange not to share this special time with my little ones, especially as the twins were just starting to understand what it was all about, but I talked to them every few days and they all seemed well and happy. So I made the best of things, enjoying my time with Iiro and counting the days until I was reunited with the children.

The Last Time

"At one of the schools we went to, the kids had prepared birthday cards for you. It was tough not to cry when they came up and handed me the pink and blue cards."

LETTER THIRTEEN

Mario and I had reached an uneasy standstill. It seemed that we were getting used to the divorce and trying to find a mutually acceptable way to handle the situation.

There were no more angry emails and Mario now called and spoke to the children regularly. I was a bit on edge, always expecting something to happen, but hoping at the same time that he had accepted the situation. I did not go as far as thinking that he would become more amicable towards me yet but that, with time, he would be able to direct a phrase or two my way without any anger so we could be in a room together for the important milestones in our kids' lives.

Divorce is never easy, and children, no matter what age, always take the brunt of it. Even though it didn't seem to affect their moods too much – and I didn't see any extreme disturbance in their behaviour – I was sure that they must have felt discomfort and instability in their lives.

At the beginning of 2017 I was enjoying being with the kids back in Cape Town. The summer in South Africa runs from December to March so we spent the weekends at my mother's apartment at Clifton Beach. Since she wasn't there, the place was usually let out on Airbnb so I timed my visits when no one was using it. Clifton lies on the Atlantic Coast and though impossibly beautiful with its white sandy beach, rocky coves and rugged coastline, the water is icy cold and the waves very rough for small children. However César ran in and out, just to get his legs wet, and had a blast without a care in the world.

The twins took some time to get used to it so they were more cautious than their older brother. It was always a lot of hassle to go anywhere with three young children but the twins were getting better at walking for extended periods. Not having to carry them around helped a lot. Maximo and Octavia watched their brother playing in the waves with great interest, admiring his spirit of adventure. These two screamed when they got a little sand on their feet and hands so they spent most of their time sitting on the towel. *It will only be a matter of time before they are also running in and out of the waves too*, I thought, lying back on a beach towel with the sun on my face.

The twins preferred the beach at Hout Bay where it was easier for them to run into the water. Though they weren't swimming yet, they splashed and played happily in the shallow waters, dragging themselves along as a play 'swim'. They even met some of their friends there, which was lovely.

I could see they were now starting to show clearer preferences for toys. Before, it didn't matter what toys they had, Octavia could be with a car and Maximo with a figurine. Now Maximo always had his Lightning McQueen car, and Octavia was becoming more girly, playing with figurines and a doll she liked to push around in a pram.

Even though the differences were starting to become more obvious, they played so well together. Maximo was usually relatively easy-going but was getting more comfortable saying 'no' and putting his foot down, but always ever so gently. He didn't always allow Octavia to get her own way these days. And she was also much better. Normally she was headstrong, but she was becoming more flexible and accepting when Maximo said 'no'. I hoped that would one day be the case with me too – Octavia and I frequently butted heads!

At night, César read to the babies. *Tsk… I shouldn't call them that anymore. Maybe the little hooligans? The things that those two get up to!* I loved to see them sitting on the kitchen sofa, one on either side of César, listening intently, while I cooked dinner and enjoyed the peace and quiet. Although they played well together, there was always some shouting. Usually by them, but once in a while I joined in as well, like the time I found them playing with a 2kg flour bag, happily distributing its contents across the kitchen floor.

They were covered in flour from head to toe, and painting with it on the floor as the dogs happily licked it clean. I only left the room for a minute! How they got the flour everywhere in such a short space of time was beyond me. I have to admit I did shout then and the twins were so surprised it gave them a fright. They did not enjoy bath time that night. It felt like it went on forever, trying to get the flour – now a paste – out of their hair.

In February I took them for their first haircut. I always shaved off Maximo's hair to a number three or so, just like César. But I hadn't touched Octavia's hair until now, nervous about handling scissors close to a constantly moving head. Besides, the little hair she did have was extremely fine. Finally, it was long enough to need a trim so I took them both to a salon in Constantia Village.

First up were César and Maximo. That was relatively quick and easy. Maximo saw how César did it and was quite happy to follow suit. Octavia, however, was bored and restless and wanted to leave. It was a challenge to persuade her into the chair and in the end I had to bribe her with chocolate, but the salon did a great job. She was not happy being told to sit still all that time but once it was done, she was really proud of her new haircut. She looked so lovely with her hair in a bob.

Now the twins were older it was easier to take them along and do more things that César also enjoyed. For Vicky's birthday we sailed on a catamaran to Camps Bay to see the sunset. The twins were a bit scared of the motion of the waves at first but relaxed after a while. We took some great pictures of them sitting on either side of me with their life vests on, talking to each other and making faces.

We often went to the waterslides in Muizenberg, which they loved, although they only wanted to go with me on the small slide, while César wanted me to go with him on the bigger ones. That was the trouble with having three – I was always outnumbered and had to be careful to give out my time and attention in equal measures. It was a bit of a juggling act but they loved the water and only came out when their lips started to turn blue.

We took to eating ice cream by the pool at home and biking in the local bike park. The twins did very well on their balance bikes and watched admiringly as César zoomed around on his big bike with pedals. He loved that they looked up to him. There were squabbles, of course, but they felt like the normal sibling stuff and never got out of hand.

They spent so much time playing together it was inevitable there would be fights, especially when César brought out his nerf guns. Really, the twins were too young for this sort of play. They didn't have the strength yet in their little fingers to pull the triggers and were not happy when César shot and hit them, especially Maximo, who always came screaming when he was used as target practice. But on the whole they were all great pals and I took tonnes of pictures and videos all summer long, never realising I would come to treasure these precious mementoes so much. Bittersweet memories, reminders that their last few months were filled with so much play, laughter and love.

Mario had decided to visit the kids in Cape Town in March. He would be in the country for three weeks and it was my responsibility to find and pay for a place for them all to stay. I wanted a place in Hout Bay near the beach but could not find one for the dates that he wanted. Eventually I found a complex a short walk away from the beach behind a mall. César was excited at the prospect of spending time with his father and being able to make friends with the other kids at the Princess Beach estate. It wasn't a big flat, but not much was needed really. Everyone had their room, there was a small cosy kitchen and living area.

On March 17, the day Mario arrived, I picked up Maximo and Octavia from school, then went home to pack all their things. By the time I was done it must have seemed like we were moving, because with their three bikes and suitcases the car was full.

On the way to the apartment I collected César from a birthday party at Clay Café. He was excited to see his father and hurriedly said goodbye to his friends. At the estate I took all their stuff up to the apartment. It took me a couple of trips, with Maximo hanging onto my leg, but not crying. He was hesitant but not as bad as previous times. Octavia was also a bit shy but seemed fine. César was all over his father.

Once I had all their stuff in the apartment, I realised that Mario had not done any shopping. His plane had arrived at 11am so I did not understand what would have taken him so long to get things sorted. He told me that there was no WiFi, so I went across the road to a store to get a portable router and some basic groceries for the kids' dinner and breakfast.

Mario had agreed that Sadi could help him out at the flat. Her presence gave me great peace of mind. I said goodbye to them and they happily started to watch something on their screens. I hadn't planned it that way but thought that it might be better that they were distracted while I left. The twins seemed to be happy to be with their father.

It was the last time I would see them alive.

Take a Knife

"I love you both so much. It is a great comfort to believe in the afterlife and know that you are well and at peace, that there is no fear or pain, just love."

LETTER FOURTEEN

It was the morning of April 6, the day I was due to pick up the kids, and I was towelling off after a shower when Mario called via Skype. I didn't pick up immediately but called back a few minutes later. Strangely, he appeared to be sitting in the dark. I wasn't due to pick up the children until 1pm.

'Why don't you come here earlier?' he suggested. 'Then we can fetch César from school and spend some time together. We can go and get ice cream so the kids can see us being together.'

He sounded a bit distant and with the curtains drawn, I couldn't see anything but I was delighted with his suggestion. Perhaps we were finally moving towards a place where we could spend an hour in each other's company, though I wondered why he had made a video call in the dark. It seemed a bit staged.

'Yes, okay,' I agreed. 'Well, first I have to do something quickly and then I'll come. Maybe 12.45pm.'

'If you can't come any earlier there's no point.'

'Okay, fine. I'll come at 12.30.'

He seemed happy with that so I finished doing what I needed to do and got ready to leave. I was surprised to see Sadi at the house. She said Mario had told her she was not needed at the flat, but she could return in three hours to do some ironing and cleaning. I told her to forget it, she didn't need to do his ironing on the last day.

I left the house at around 12.15pm. It had been a long time since I'd seen the kids. In the last three weeks I'd filled the hours with exercise, enjoying my time alone and some creative projects. Iiro also came to see me during this time, and his parents visited from Finland. They met the kids as well a couple of days before Mario arrived.

After leaving the kids with their father we took Iiro's parents on a road trip through the vineyards in our region. It was lovely to spend quality time with them and get to know each other better. I'd been in touch with the children every three or four days. César was always fine when we spoke and so was Octavia. Maximo was the only one who said he missed me but this was to be expected – he was my sensitive little boy and I knew it must be hard to be without his Mama for such a long period.

I made a point not to drive by Hout Bay during this period as it would make it more difficult for the children if they saw me. But as the holidays neared the end, I got more and more excited about being reunited with them all again. I arrived a little after 12.30pm, parked and went up to the apartment, longing to hug the twins and César after not having held them in my arms for three weeks.

Mario opened the door before I even got a chance to knock. He put his finger to his lips to signify that I should be quiet and, in a low voice said: 'Don't make a noise. The babies are asleep.' I walked in and placed some washing on the bar counter. As I did, I noticed several kitchen knives laid out on the counter. *What a strange thing to do, leaving knives around where the twins would be able to reach them.* I dismissed it as I was taking the children home with me soon anyway.

'Did they have a difficult night?' I asked as I sat down on the couch, placing my bag at my feet. This wasn't their usual nap time.

'Yes,' he replied. He was quiet and just looked at me.

'So, why did you ask me to come early? Just to look at me or do you want to talk?'

'I want to talk. I want to make your life as difficult as you have made mine.' My heart skipped a beat and my legs felt weak. Would he try to get custody of the kids?

'Recently, or since the divorce?' I asked steadily.

'For everything, for the whole divorce… You will soon see.'

I had no response to this, and I didn't want to argue, so I did not say anything. I was dumbfounded again. I thought that we had turned a corner, that we could move forward and be civil to each other for the sake of the children. How many times did he have to prove me wrong until I understood that he would not change? All my hopeful thinking was pointless. He got up and went to the kitchen and I shook my head in frustration. *How stupid I've been!* Now, as I turned around on the sofa I saw that he had picked up one of the big kitchen knives. I stood up, confused.

'Pick up a knife and kill me with it because I am going to kill you.'

He spoke calmly, with no emotion, his voice flat. He did not shout. There was no menace. His face was like stone. He held the knife low at his side, next to his thigh. There were no other sounds, it was like someone had pressed pause, and only he was talking. My whole focus was on his face, and that knife. I was trying to make sense of what he was saying. Everything else disappeared.

I tried to read him, to see if there was a glimmer, a hint of a smile, anything to let me know that this was a cruel joke, his way of making me pay.

Nothing.

His eyes were dark, unreadable and unmoving. He stood there and repeated the words: 'Take a knife and kill me, because I will kill you.'

My confusion slowly turned to panic. I could not understand why he was saying that, or what he was planning to do.

'What are you doing?' I asked, in a near whisper. 'The kids are asleep. You'll wake them up.'

He then uttered the words that pierced the fog in my brain and shook me to my core: 'No, the kids are dead.'

What? No. No, it can't be true. It can't be true.

I put my hand over his hand that was holding the knife. I didn't think about it, I just found my hand on top of his. He did not move. His hand felt strong and unwavering around the hilt of the blade. I realised that I would not be able to fight him. He seemed lifeless in a way, but the strength I could feel in the hand with the knife was immovable. What unnerved me most was the calm way he again said: 'Take a knife and kill me because I will kill you.'

Everything seemed lifeless, as if the air had been sucked out of the room.

For a moment, I was uncertain what to do. I wasn't scared for my own safety but terrified of a darker intent beneath his cold exterior. Something inside told me to move quickly. *I have to see my babies, to make sure that they are alright.* I turned around to run up the stairs. Out of the corner of my eye I saw that he had grabbed my bag. In my confused state I turned back and tried to take it back from him. But he had a firm grip on it and I was not able to pry it from him. *The bag doesn't matter*, my mind cried, *go and check on your babies.*

I ran up the stairs and saw the two single beds. The twins were lying on their backs, their bodies covered by blankets up to their necks, only their little faces showing. A fleeting thought crossed my mind that they were not the twins at all, but dolls made to look like them.

Octavia's head was turned to the side, her cheek blue from the blood that had collected there. Maximo had blood bubbles in his mouth. I took four steps closer to them. Maximo's stomach was making a gurgling sound which terrified me, but at the same time it gave me hope that they were still alive. I pulled the covers off and touched them all over.

They were cold, unresponsive, stiff and unmoving. I realised they had been here for some time. Meanwhile, Mario had followed me up to the room with the knife.

'What did you do?' I said to him. 'What did you do?'

He didn't respond.

'César! Where is César?'

'He's fine.'

I went back to my babies. I touched them again to see if they had visible injuries. I picked up Octavia. She was as stiff as a board. I laid her next to Maximo so that I could touch them at the same time. I kept touching them, telling them to wake up, repeating: 'No puede ser. No puede ser' (It can't be. It can't be). How could he have done this? It didn't feel real, it couldn't be real. I started to cry softly. It never occurred to me to call out for help. I was devastated. *My babies were dead.* All thoughts of Mario with the knife were gone. I only focused on the twins.

I don't know how much time passed. I seemed to have slipped into another dimension, a state where nothing mattered except the two still bodies in front of me. Mario came up to the room once or twice maybe, I wasn't sure. I was so engulfed by despair I was barely aware of his presence. *I had left them with their father – they should have been safe. How could he have done such a thing? Oh, my babies! My little babies.*

Slowly it dawned on me that I had to get out of there. I had to make sure that César was safe. There was no way I could go out the front door. Mario would not let me leave without a fight, he had made that clear, and I was certain that I wouldn't win in any confrontation with him. So now I opened the bedroom window to see if I could escape that way. We were four storeys up but the window opened onto the roof so now I took off my shoes and climbed out of the window, clambering upwards until I was straddling the roof, one leg dangling on either side.

My eyes darted back to the open window, desperately hoping he hadn't come up the stairs again to find me missing. I didn't have long before he realised what I was doing. Now I crawled along the roof of the building.

The apartment was on one corner of a small estate and I could see that, on the ground at the far side of the estate, a man was washing his car. I tried to get his attention by waving my arms, but I was too far away for him to notice me. I did not cry out, scared of drawing Mario's attention. *If I make it across to the other side of the roof, I can jump onto the landing below where there are stairs down to ground level.*

I edged my way to the verge of the roof and slowly let myself down on the drainpipe, sliding down on my stomach. My dress caught on the roof gutter and for a moment I just hung there, my dress pulled up around my waist. *Please don't let anyone come out of the door now*, I thought, as I dangled, half-naked in front of an apartment front door. *Shit, there's nothing else for it.* I let myself drop and pulled my dress free.

I stumbled down the stairs, worried my legs were shaking too much to be able to run fast. I needed to get to the gates of the compound and escape before he came after me with the knife. I kept looking back over my shoulder. *Is he following me?* Then, as I ran into the main courtyard in front of the apartments I noticed my car was gone. He must have taken it. At the main gate I saw the guard.

'Did Mario leave with my car?' I panted.

'Yes.'

'You have to call the police,' I said. 'Call the police because he killed the twins.'

For a moment the guard seemed too shocked to respond.

'What? What do you mean? I see him with the twins all the time. Today! I saw them today.'

'He killed them. Please. Call the police now. He might be going to fetch my other son.'

The guard must have sensed my terror because he called the police. Then I asked to use his phone to contact the school. But it was not a smart phone and I didn't know the number of the school off by heart. By now I was sobbing uncontrollably and between my tears and the panic, I couldn't figure out how to find the number.

As I was floundering in despair and unsure of what to do, a woman stopped her car by the gate and got out to help.

I do not remember much about her. I was in such despair that the only thing that stuck to me was her kind and peaceful presence. I think she had blonde hair and seemed older than I was. Or maybe that was just the impression I had of her because she seemed to help make me feel safe. I slumped on the ground as the pain overtook me. Now I felt I was able to let go and I totally broke down as deep wrenching sobs overtook me.

'She says her husband has killed their twins in the apartment,' the guard explained.

'I... need to call the school... to make sure my son is safe.' I gasped.

She asked for the name of the school, Googled it and handed me the phone once it was ringing.

Gemma, the school secretary, answered.

'Is César still there?' I asked, my voice thick with emotion.

'I think so…' she replied. 'But I'll go and check…'

In a matter of seconds she was back on the line: 'Yes, he's here.'

Oh thank God! I was so relieved I broke down completely.

'Don't let Mario take him,' I managed to say before handing the phone back to the woman. Now the tears just would not stop. I sat on the ground as the pain overtook me. The woman placed a hand on my shoulder and quietly spoke: 'Lord, watch over this woman, this mother. Be with her, stay with her. Give her strength in this, her darkest hour…'

The words washed over me like a balm. I'm not religious but at that moment I felt immense gratitude for her help and her support. I was not alone. There was someone here for me, helping me, taking care of me. For that, I would always be grateful.

'How? How could he do it?' I gasped through the tears.

I didn't understand. They were his own children. Guilt flooded in.

'I left them somewhere unsafe.'

'You couldn't have known,' she said. 'You could never have known.'

After what felt like an eternity the police arrived. It was now around 1.30pm. They asked me what had happened and what my car model, make and licence number was so they could get an APB out on Mario. I had just recently memorised my licence plate as I could never remember it. A few weeks before a parking attendant had asked me for the number. When I told him that I didn't know it, he asked me how long I had been driving the car. When I said four years he replied: 'Then you should know the number.'

He was right, so I memorised it. I told the police what they needed to know, repeating myself a couple of times to make myself understood. Then a policewoman walked with me to the apartment.

They had to force their way into the flat as Mario had locked the door and the security gate. Once the police saw that I was telling the truth, they took me back to the bottom of the stairs to wait. By this stage I was inconsolable. They brought me a blanket and sugar water. I saw paramedics come and go. *Maybe… just maybe…*

'Is it true?' I asked the policewoman. 'Are my babies really dead?'

Perhaps I had made a mistake. Perhaps they could be saved. For a second I allowed myself to hope.

'Yes, I'm afraid the paramedics pronounced them dead at 14.09,' she replied.

And my heart shattered into tiny little pieces.

A volunteer at the police station and a counsellor for victims came to give me support. Caroline, a name similar to my sister's, was a great help. Her kids went to the same school as César, so she contacted them to make sure César was there and told them to phone Vicky's husband Johan, to ask him to pick César up as Vicky was in Spain for business meetings.

Precious Scars

She asked me if I knew the telephone numbers of family members to notify them of what had happened. I managed to call home. Sadi came on the phone, and I asked to speak to Iiro. All I was able to get out was that Mario had killed the twins. I started crying uncontrollably so Caroline took the phone to explain the situation to him.

At some point I think the police showed me my bag and asked if it was mine. When I confirmed it, they asked if I could tell them what was inside. Once I did, they were able to verify that Mario had taken my car keys and phone.

My sister Carolin and Iiro arrived a bit later. Carolin, who was pregnant with her first child, was in the country on a visit and staying with us. I wasn't able to tell them much. After a while, the counsellor suggested I see a doctor. Apparently I was covered in scrapes and bruises from my descent down the roof ledge, though I wasn't aware of any injuries on my body.

The doctor looked me over, cleaned my wounds and prescribed Valium to help calm me down. By now I was shaking all over and freezing cold. He said it was shock. Caroline took us home while my sister Carolin stayed at the scene, as a family member had to be there. After being at home for a while, I decided I was composed enough to see César. *He needs to hear this from me, no one else.*

At Vicky's house I found César playing in the gym on a small trampoline.

'Come with me, I need to tell you something,' I took his hand and we went to the guest bedroom and sat on the bed. There was no other way to do this – I had to tell it to him straight.

'Your father killed the twins,' I said slowly.

It never occurred to me to shield him in any way from what happened. I thought that he would hear things from other people at school and wanted him to find out from me, not from a stranger or another child who would have picked it up from another adult. I wanted him to know the truth as I knew it.

Maybe I did him a disservice, but I did not want him to feel that I was keeping things from him. We were also going to be talking about this within the family, and I did not want him to feel like we were keeping things from him if we suddenly went quiet when he entered a room. I would not give him any unnecessary details, but the facts. I would not want to be protected from information from others, I would want to know. He is obviously much younger so what I tell him I tried to give it to him in an age-appropriate way.

He was shocked at first, not sure whether to believe my words, but then he looked at my face. By now I had cried so much my eyes were puffy and my cheeks stained with tears. It was clear to him that this was true. His face crumpled and he burst into tears.

'How? How did they die?' he wept.

I didn't know at this point. I'd seen no knife wounds or marks on their neck so I made an assumption.

'They were given something to make them fall asleep and not wake up.'

'Why did Papi do that?'

'I don't know how he could have done it but he said he wanted to make me suffer.'

It broke my heart to see César like this. There was so much pain, shock and incomprehension on that small face. He was only seven years old.

We talked for a little while. I'm not sure what about, but he told me straight away that he wanted me to grow another baby so that he had someone to play with.

'And I want Iiro to stay forever,' he added. 'He shouldn't leave.'

I cried and that upset him further.

'I don't want to see you cry, Mama. Please don't cry.'

'Okay, okay…' I said, trying to soothe him.

'Shall we go home?' I said eventually.

'No,' he shook his head. 'I don't want to go home. I don't want to be on my own.'

I understood and agreed to let him stay at Vicky's house to be with his cousins. It was probably best for him to stay here, giving me time to grieve without having to hide it from him.

Back at home, I didn't know what to do with myself. At some point, I wandered into the twins' room. *They should be here, playing and exploring the new beds I'd made for them as a surprise.* It was a castle, with a turret in the middle and the two beds at either side. Last night, I had put new sheets on the beds, imagining the delight on their faces when they caught sight of the castle for the first time. *How they would have loved climbing up from the centre to play princess and knight!* It struck me now that they would never even see their new beds.

When Carolin returned home she was with Juan Smuts. He said he had been to Princess Beach to make sure that the police were doing everything correctly and was now here to get a record of what had happened. I told him, through sobs, and Iiro and Carolin were there to hear the dreadful sequence of events. I was grateful at least that I did not have to repeat it. Meanwhile, the police called to say Mario had been caught. He was found close to the M3 in the residential suburb of Tokai. They had first located my car and spotted him walking towards Cape Town. When he realised that they were after him, he started to run back to the car but they intercepted him. He had knife wounds in his abdomen and scratches on the sides of his neck. My phone was missing. The police later said that a knife from the kitchen was missing, but they could not find it in his possession so he must have thrown it away at some point. They also found loose cash, a passport, a white BlackBerry and bank cards on him. He was arrested and taken to Victoria hospital in Wynberg where he was kept on suicide watch.

After Juan and his secretary left, I felt like I needed to get my mind off everything so I tried watching TV but it was all a blur. It was all too much. I needed to escape from this unbearable pain and took a Valium pill, prescribed by the doctor. I managed to eat a little food Johan brought over, chicken curry with rice. Funny how odd details like this stood out in my mind while the rest of the time seemed to seep away into nothingness. Eventually the Valium started to kick in and weariness overtook me. I went to bed and shut my eyes against the horrors of the day. But my sleep was fitful and I kept waking up, my mind back in the bedroom where I had found them.

Their still, lifeless bodies lying peacefully side by side.

PART TWO
AFTER

"Life can only be understood backwards, but it must be lived forward."

Søren Kierkegaard

"Time is a dressmaker specialising in alterations."

Faith Baldwin

The Funeral

"When I think of you two, I have a moment of utter despair before the sadness and tears come. When the tears don't come, there is sometimes more despair, but every so often it's a little lighter."

LETTER EIGHTEEN

The next day went on forever. I had an appointment at the police station at 11am to give my statement and it felt like it took hours. One thought kept going over and over in my mind: *my babies are gone.* Nevertheless, I wanted to give my statement clearly, to make it as detailed and accurate as possible as I knew it would affect the trial in the future. The process was slow.

The captain asked me a question, then wrote down my answer. Methodically, we got through the series of events that led up to this moment. At least it gave me plenty of time to recollect and remember everything. At some point, Vicky arrived. I hadn't seen her until now because she was in Spain on family business. She came straight to the police station and we shared an emotional hug, then left so that I could continue giving my statement. I heard her crying outside.

The Funeral

My God, this will affect so many people's lives.

That afternoon we returned to Vicky's house, now our base camp, for lunch. The world seemed to swirl around me in a blur – people, places and conversations merging into one ill-defined cloud of activity. For some reason the food on my plate came to me in clear detail: chicken wraps with avocado, a tomato salad and cheese.

People spoke to me but I barely heard them, my mind speeding in a million directions at once. *Why hadn't I known what Mario was up to? Could I have prevented it? How was César coping? Did they suffer? Did they know?* Endless questions with no answers. I kept going back to the last day I spent with them. I should have hugged them tighter, given them another kiss. I should not have let them go. I should have kept them from harm.

Juan Smuts came to talk to the family about what the next year would look like for me. He said I would be giving evidence and needed patience as it would take a long time before this was over. At one stage we talked about the near future and the case against Mario. It was hard to take in what he was saying. It felt as if I was moving through a thick fog the whole time.

Time concertinaed; at times compressing, racing ahead of me, at other times extending so much that it felt as if all the clocks had stopped. I lost a sense of the days and hours passing. You hear about loved ones having an intuition when something terrible happens. An unseen connection so powerful that they *know* when that person is in trouble, they feel their loved ones leaving this earth. *I didn't know. Why didn't*

Precious Scars

I know? Maybe I wasn't good enough a mother to have that connection with them. I had left them with their father, I had left them somewhere unsafe.

At times it was hard to stop the guilt from overwhelming me. My mind kept returning to the last day I spent with them. They had been alive for three weeks after I last saw them and I hadn't been able to experience that. I hadn't seen them or talked to them a lot. It felt strange that even though they had been here I hadn't been with them.

The days merged. My family were all here, helping to look after César, helping to organise the funeral. We were all seated at Vicky's massive dining room table for dinner one day – Vicky and her family, my sister Carolin, my parents, Ana with her partner, Iiro, César and I – when my father looked up and said: 'Well, we are still a big family,' and burst out crying. I thought I should go and hug him, but I was too numb, and my thinking too slow. I still regret that I didn't.

Vicky had recommended I see a psychologist and I asked her to call a friend as I wanted to see someone I was familiar with. I did not feel like going to a stranger. It felt safer and more at ease. Gary Viljoen was perfect. I did not know him well, but enough not to feel uncomfortable. I was not really sure how I would cope talking to a psychologist. It was the first time for me but I knew that I needed to.

Two days after they were killed, we got word from Juan Smuts that we could go and identify the babies. The family suggested that I should not go as it would be too awful. But I had to. When I climbed out of that window, I did not say goodbye. I just left. I had to make sure one more time that it had really happened, that it was them, and that they were gone.

Iiro and my parents came with me. We had to wait at the undertakers first for the papers to be processed. After what seemed like an eternity, a staff member led us through the door to a corridor that led to two separate viewing rooms. I imagined I would be able to see and stand next to them but they were behind a glass door a few metres away.

We saw Octavia first, her hair was wet from the autopsy, but she was no longer blue. Maximo's hair was also wet, but there were no blood bubbles. They both looked sunken somehow, so tiny, lonely and cold. So forlorn. I felt forlorn too, like something inside me had been taken away and I had no idea if it would ever come back. I stood there for a minute, looking at the children I had brought into this world, their small bodies no longer growing, the milestones forever unreached. 'Goodbye,' I said quietly to each child. I couldn't stop the tears. 'I'm sorry. I'm so very sorry.'

After I had composed myself, the undertakers asked me some questions about the babies and their last few weeks, and whether they were on any medication. I explained that when I had dropped off the kids they had the sniffles so I had left Mario with the basic medical stuff like cough syrup and Nurofen. I didn't know then what the police had found in the flat and they didn't tell me until I was eliminated from their enquiries. We went back to Vicky's that day and after a dinner of mashed potatoes with meat, pepper sauce and beans, we went home. It had been a trying day and though I was exhausted, sleep evaded me.

A couple of days later we went for a walk. I didn't feel like going – I didn't feel like doing anything – but I knew it would be good for me to get out and I obliged César to come with us. He hated it and complained the whole way. I could see his anger boiling over, guilt and sadness fuelling his fury.

'Where are the babies now?' he demanded to know.

'They are in heaven.'

'What is heaven? Where is it?'

'It's somewhere in the sky where you are happy, have no pain, and are with friends or family who have gone before. It is a place where you can do what you want.'

I wanted to answer him as truthfully as possible in a way he could understand, to share with him the way I understood it.

'Well, I also want to be able to choose what I want to do,' he reasoned. 'They get to have everything they want and I don't. I want to go to heaven too.'

Oh, my child!

'César, no. You can't go there yet,' I say sadly.

'Why not?'

'It's not… erm.. it's not somewhere you can just go if you choose.'

I was floundering. Iiro now stepped in, trying to explain to César that heaven was very far away from your loved ones on earth and once there, you couldn't come back again. *This is too hard for us.* César would also need to speak with someone. A professional. We would all need a lot of help.

There were times I zoned out into another world, staring at nothing for I don't know how long and then coming round, like waking up, unaware of how much time had passed. I needed to get back a sense of reality, to be able to be in a place where I could help César in his time of need. I could see that he was spiralling downwards, scared to leave me, frightened that I would suddenly disappear too. And then, what would happen to him? His father now gone, I was all he had and he clung to me with terror.

I thought about his future and how much this would shape the rest of his life. Would he wonder at some point about his genes and what he might have inherited from his father? Before, he had adored Mario. Now he said that he hated him. He was angry and it would probably get worse. *He does not understand how Mario could have done what he did. How could he, if even I don't understand?*

I made an appointment for César to see a therapist, the same one he had seen during the divorce. He didn't want to go at first, unwilling even to leave the house.

'What if people ask me about it? I don't want to cry in front of them.'

We had a very solemn birthday for Mama on April 11, she didn't want any singing. We went for a walk on the beach and then lunch. It felt surreal to be in a restaurant, doing something so normal after something so catastrophic. Could we really go out into the world as if nothing had changed? No one felt like celebrating but we forced ourselves to do these things.

Although I don't think I was much of a pleasure to be around, interaction compelled me to do something other than dwell on the twins and the lives they had been robbed of. For just a very short while I stopped thinking of all the things they would never do or experience.

César didn't want to go back to school. He was afraid of breaking down in front of the other students so his teachers, Sharon and Julia, the school counsellor, and Gill, the Vice Principal, came to visit. They assured him that if he needed help they were there for him and explained they had put a tent in the classroom where he could go and be by himself. This tent was only for him, it was to be his safe zone. He seemed to like the idea and after the visit was more relaxed about going back.

The new school term after the Easter holidays started a few days later and Iiro and I took César to school that first day. He was a bit apprehensive but seemed to perk up when he saw his friends and the tent in the classroom. I was pleased that I'd been able to take him and not break down but nervous as we drove away that morning. It had been a little over two weeks since the twins' death. *Was it too soon? Would he be alright?*

I made an appointment with Sam, my tarot card reader and counsellor. As soon as we saw one another, we both broke down.

'I'm so sorry I didn't see this coming,' she said. I had last visited her on March 28. I'm not sure what I would have done if she had told me then something was going to happen. Would I have gone to Mario and demanded he give me the twins? Or tell the police that a clairvoyant had told me the father of my children was going to harm them? It would not have helped.

The Funeral

'What I do know is that they went peacefully and felt no fear or pain,' she said. 'They don't remember anything after they had their breakfast and drank a bitter milk that Mario made them. There was no pain and they left quickly.'

I wept with relief. It was so important for me to hear that. Sam said they were now playing happily and were at peace.

'They want to hang around until César's birthday and then they will move on,' she explained. They had asked her for some Nesquik, which they loved drinking at home, and asked her to buy two trees for me.

'Maximo wants an olive tree, but Octavia is taking a while to choose,' Sam frowned. I smiled ruefully. That was typical of my daughter!

'She doesn't want a lemon tree…' Sam is saying slowly, as if listening to the words. *Clever girl, as we already have three.* 'Okay, she has finally decided on another olive tree.'

For a moment I felt a pang of jealousy that Sam could hear my children and I could not.

'But they can always hear you,' Sam consoled me. 'They are always around you.'

Sam said the twins wanted the trees planted next to each other in the small playground in our garden.

'They said that they want you to have another child,' she added. That was the second time I had been asked to have another child… both requests from my children. But I couldn't imagine it at this time. It broke my heart just thinking about it.

It never occurred to me to stop believing. I think because it helped me to cling to something that would ultimately help me understand or at least accept. I did not see it then, but I realised that bad things happen to everyone. There is no escape, sooner or later you will be affected by death. Realising that their suffering had a finality helped me. It was just mine I had to get through.

Seeing Sam was bittersweet. After I left I had a feeling for the first time that I would get through this. As terrible as it was, as unbearable as it felt at times I knew that with all the help, support and encouragement from everyone around me, I would survive. There was no other way. Mario had broken my heart, but I would find peace and happiness again. In my diary that night I wrote:

I will miss my babies for the rest of my life, and wonder what they would look like, and be like, and what they would have done with their lives. I have to get used to a different way of life, one that includes grief so deep that it seems I will never recover. But I will not give him the satis-faction, especially since César needs and deserves a mother who is there for him 100%.

I am not sure where I got this strength from. It was just something that I realised I could not allow myself to change in a negative way. It was just there. It was like realising that I had a backbone, and this was it.

At some point during this time I cleaned out their rooms. Vicky warned me that I should not do it too soon and she was probably right. I would have kept more of their things if I had not done the clean-out so quickly. But it was hard to see their toys and clothes all over the kitchen and piled up in their room. Their bedroom was right next to the kitchen so I was reminded of their absence every time I walked past. I felt like I needed to put their things away. Maybe it was a way of moving forward.

One of the hardest things I had to let go of were the bunnies Vicky had bought for the twins before they were born, a black one for Maximo and one with a white forehead and chest for Octavia. So soft. They loved them so and carried them everywhere. I decided that they should go in their coffins to keep them company. It was incredibly sad, but I felt it would help in some way. It would have been worse seeing those bunnies lying on their beds, waiting to be cuddled by their owners.

My sisters organised the funeral. I couldn't do it. The one thing I wanted to do was to make the memorial card, choosing a wonderful photo of them both smiling, sitting next to each other for the cover. I wanted to find something to write on it, but nothing I read online resonated, so I decided to write something myself. It took me a while to get my head into gear. It felt like I was wading through mud. In the end, this is what I came up with:

> *"Together you came into this world*
> *Together you left.*
> *My hands can no longer touch you,*
> *Nor my arms embrace you.*
> *My lips won't be able to kiss you*
> *Or tell you*
> *"I love you"*
> *But in my heart, you will remain*
> *Forever."*

Precious Scars

The night before the cremation on April 13 I couldn't sleep. At around 4am I got out of bed, determined to find something to do that would be tedious enough not to require brain concentration but that would occupy my hands and stop me thinking. But I couldn't watch TV or read a book. I had no focus. Instead, I just sat in the kitchen staring into space, trying not to imagine how the day would unfold. It would all just happen anyway.

Carolin left to pick up the memorial card from the printers and some bracelets that she had made as a memory for the family and those who had been part of the twins' lives. Marga came home with Adele, the twins' teacher at their pre-school, and took Sadi and Moses. Then we all went to Vicky's house to drive together to Maitland Road Crematorium. Before I left, I took half a Valium as I could feel myself slowly slipping into anxiousness and despair.

The chapel was in the middle of the cemetery, not as picturesque as I would like to imagine it, but the interior was small and lovely. As soon as I walked in, I saw the two tiny coffins at the end, near the altar, and I broke down. Just to see a child's coffin, any child's coffin, is heartbreaking, even if you didn't know them. I couldn't imagine what this must have been like for the rest of the family. César wanted to see the children's faces, but I explained that it wouldn't be a good idea as they would not look like they did when they were alive, and that it would be best to remember them as they were.

The family gave a few short speeches, but I could not hear anything. It was all too much and I felt myself zoning in and out of reality. We laid flowers on the caskets. I played one of their favourite songs, *Fireball* by Pitbull. It was one of their three favourites; the others were *Let it Go* from Frozen and *Gangnam Style* (which I refused to play unless absolutely necessary.) César and I tried to sing along to *Fireball*, especially when the song came to a crescendo, but it was tough. I realised that singing was something that I was unable to do, I would start crying immediately. Singing is something you do with feeling, and I could not.

After the ceremony we went back to Vicky's house. Friends and family began arriving very soon to pay their condolences. When I saw the mother of Indiana and Arizona, twins who had been friends of my two, I started crying. She was also upset.

Once everyone was inside Vicky made a speech that was sweet and heartfelt, but I didn't hear most of it, because Vicky was crying too hard while she talked, as I was. Afterwards she came to hug me and I told her I had struggled to hear her. Everyone was quiet. I suppose it must have been just as bad for all those present. Vicky said that as no one had understood her she would print the speech and hand it out. People laughed and it broke the silence and people started to make small talk.

Later we signed a little card and tied it to white balloons to send the children a message. The balloons were biodegradable with seeds in them so fynbos shrubs would start growing in the places they landed. It was beautiful watching them all fly up into the air, so peaceful and angelic, getting smaller and smaller as they fled through the air. Soon, just tiny specks in the distance. And I wanted to go home.

The funeral had been surreal and I was glad it was over. I felt pleased that so many people had come to support and show their love, but it was exhausting spending so much time making small talk.

At the end of it all, I just felt like locking myself away, although what awaited me at home were all the bittersweet memories that were just as hard to face. Right now it was difficult to be anywhere at all. On one hand it was difficult to be with people and make conversation. On the other hand being on my own was worse. There was nowhere I felt at peace when my head and heart were in such torment.

Everyone in my family had come to South Africa. Carolin's boyfriend, Jeff, had flown in from America. He had been of great help to her at the scene of the crime, instructing her to call the lawyer, our parents and other two sisters, to let them know what had happened. It can't have been easy for her to have to tell the story over and over again to friends and family, who were probably experiencing confusion and heartbreak on the other end of the line. All my family had put their own lives on hold to spend time giving me support before and after the funeral. Having them here meant the world to me and despite the unending pain there were moments I felt grateful and genuinely blessed.

None of Mario's family were at the funeral.

I hadn't spoken to any of them since the twins were killed and nobody from his side had attempted to reach out to me either. I hardly knew what I would say to them. I didn't expect to hear from them but I felt so sorry for them. I couldn't imagine what they were going through. I kept wondering if I

The Funeral

should call them but was told that it would be best not to. It was so shocking to us all and Mario had told the police that he didn't know what had happened. The implication seemed to be that he had had some kind of mental breakdown or psychotic episode. What would they make of it all, from so far away?

Vicky had initially cancelled the annual Easter Sunday egg hunt on April 16, but I didn't want the kids to miss it. I thought that things needed to stay as 'normal' as possible, especially for César. It had become a tradition. Quite a few friends joined in, and everyone enjoyed it

It was hard, of course, knowing the babies would have loved to find the eggs and eat the chocolate. Octavia loved her chocolate and would try to get as much in as possible. Maximo as well, but Octavia was more like me in that regard. They would have been playing with many kids as well. It was hard to think about what they would be doing so I concentrated on César which helped take my mind off the twins for a bit. I was so grateful to have him, it made the weight I carried a bit more bearable.

In mid-May Iiro organised to meet some of his friends at the Park Life concert in Green Point. César also came along. It was nice to listen to music, but I was not remotely close to being able to enjoy myself yet. I met Bellie for the first time, the wife of Iiro's great friend Sam. She told me how sorry she was, and I just burst out crying. She also started to cry. I felt so miserable. I didn't want to make an event that was joyful for everyone else a sad place.

I have to get out of here. I couldn't speak, just turned around

and walked away, taking my grief from the group. I hoped I
didn't make her feel bad. I always appreciated it when people
gave condolences even though my tears often flowed. *I can't
do anything about that yet.* I had always felt awkward giving my
condolences because I could not imagine what people were
going through and feeling. Now that I was on the other end,
it wasn't any easier receiving them. I could see that people
were trying, and I appreciated it. I felt sorry for them mostly
because I knew how hard it must be.

I struggled through the days, making vague attempts to
keep up a normal routine, though the deaths had destroyed
my idea of what normal looked like. I couldn't concentrate
on anything for very long and had very little energy. I'd be
fine one minute and then something, like seeing their names
on the kitchen calendar, would set me off.

A week after the concert a friend organised a hike from
Hout Bay to Myburgh's Waterfall Ravine, a beautiful trail of
about four and a half hours with great views of Hout Bay,
Sandy Bay and Llandudno. I was thankful to be dragged out
of the house to explore the woods at the bottom of Table
Mountain, along the coastline. We picked our way through
the hilly trail, concentrating on our steps, soaking up the
beautiful scenery. I breathed in the fresh air and felt the
gentle, healing power of nature all around me, soothing my
shattered soul.

There were eight of us in total, though we didn't talk much
on the hike, at least I didn't. I didn't want to. Even when we
stopped to take a break in a cool dark cave, I preferred to
remain silent.

The Funeral

At night I wrote in my diary, letting the words spill onto the page:

We are receiving such generous support from everyone, I am so grateful. Strangely, I can't make any type of decision or remember things that do not involve the twins or César. The little energy I have is consumed by César, there is absolutely nothing left for any other part of life.

I cry on my own. I know that I don't have to hide it, and I don't do it on purpose, but I am reaching a point where I can't bear the pity and pain that I see in other people's eyes. I find that it is hard for me to keep eye contact. I am not sure if it's because I don't want to see their pain and pity or because I don't want them to see mine.

I am alone, preferring solitude right now. I should start exercising again, but I don't seem to have the energy. I am still stuck with thoughts of how this could have happened, how I had gone from being the mother to three children to only having one. I belong to a club that no one ever wants to be part of. I keep thinking that I now have to live my life without them, and I can't imagine it. I feel their loss so profoundly.

Slowly everyone moves on, keeping the babies close. Grief drags one down, moving and thinking takes that much more effort. Most days are empty and numb.

Grieving

"As I was driving back from dropping off César at school, towards my yoga lesson, I cried again, like so many other times. I miss you so much."

LETTER TWENTY-SIX

In May I learned about the car crash.

A police investigator came to the house and told me that Mario had been in an accident on the morning of the twins' murder. It happened on Main Road, Hout Bay, as he was driving from the babies' school towards the apartment they were staying. Since the twins did not have school that day we had no idea why he was on that road. Even more baffling was that, according to the driver of the lorry he collided with, Mario drove straight into him on purpose.

The driver said he looked him in the eye and then swerved directly into his path. Fortunately, no one was injured but the rental car was a total wreck. According to eye-witnesses Mario stayed inside with the twins after the collision, refusing to get out until a woman, living close to where the accident happened, offered to drive them to the apartment.

Mario insisted they were all fine and did not want to go to

hospital. That woman told the police that when they arrived at the apartment, the twins didn't want her to leave. Octavia would not let go of her leg as she tried to say goodbye.

It struck me then that Octavia realised that something was wrong, and was unhappy to be there with her father, or was scared after the accident. My heart broke when I heard that. They must have been so frightened and confused on their last day, so much so they clung to a stranger. This also explained why Mario had taken off in my car that day. Thankfully, the accident had happened after César was taken to school so he wasn't in the car at the time.

As I was discussing new developments with the police investigator, I started to feel sick in my stomach. It was all I could do to stop myself from throwing up. Was this a new psychological side effect of grief? I recalled the same thing had happened when I picked up a copy of *YOU* magazine which had an article about the murder. I hadn't read it yet as even looking at it made me queasy. It was strange that I reacted this way. I wanted to be involved and up to date with the investigation but feeling ill every time it was discussed would make that very difficult.

After the visit I thought about the car crash. *Was that Mario's first attempt? Did he also want to die? Is that why he told me to kill him? Did he hope that I would then pay for his death? And maybe for the twins as well?* I had so many questions I wanted to ask him. Why the accident, Mario? Was it your alibi, to make it appear you had lost your mind?

He had told the police that he didn't know what had happened that day. He had no memory of the events. And I knew deep down this was as much as he would ever say. He would never tell me the truth. Never. At first Mario had been in hospital for his wounds and kidney stones but he was now in prison where he was kept on suicide watch. As much as I tried not to dwell on it, the accident played on my mind.

At some point César asked to go and see his father in prison. I told him it was too soon and that we should wait and see how it went with the trial. My lawyers agreed with this, though there were many times I felt the urge to go there myself and drag answers out of him.

In the cold light of day, I could see it was a bad idea. There was no point. He wouldn't say anything and I didn't want to give him the satisfaction of seeing me broken. But if César had pressed it, I would have let him. I thought about this a lot. He still loved his father but he had questions about what he'd done. I didn't want to get in the way and I thought if seeing his father helped César to recover I'd be all for it. But I wasn't convinced it would and since I was wholly responsible for his emotional wellbeing I had to be careful not to take well-meaning steps that had every chance of backfiring.

Laurence and Brent, the founders of Zip Zap Circus, offered to dedicate a room in their new building to the twins. It was a wonderful gesture and we all agreed the Dance Room, with its mountain views, a balcony and a music storeroom attached, would be perfect. I was glad there would be something out there with their names to be remembered by friends and strangers.

It seemed so important to me, especially since they had such a short life. Zip Zap was an organisation close to my heart. Laurence and Brent started it 40 years ago, putting on circus skills classes for kids as young as six from the townships for free, performing all over Cape Town. Vicky became a trustee shortly after moving to Cape Town, helping them grow and secure funding opportunities.

César had attended classes there but the twins were too young. I love the concept of Zip Zap, building happiness, confidence and skills amongst children who had the hardest lives. It was a real force for good and I was so pleased the twins would always be associated with this positive, joyful place.

Iiro organised a lunch at home with some friends and I made my first cake since the twin's death. This felt like a mini accomplishment. It briefly crossed my mind that I should not leave it out on the table while we showed them the house after lunch but then I forgot to move it and when we came to sit down the cake was gone and our mix breed dog Shredder was slinking away, guilt all over his face.

At my session with Sam the next day, the first thing she said was that Maximo thought it hilarious that a dog had eaten the cake. I loved hearing that. I could just see and hear them laughing about it. It gave me a sense of love that was difficult to describe.

Meanwhile, I managed to find a way of being creative that wasn't too taxing, making small flowers out of wire and nail polish. They were just little ornaments, not too tricky to create, but a nice distraction for my hands and mind. I twisted the wire around my finger to make the outline shape of the petals, then wound the wire around itself downwards to form a stem.

Precious Scars

After a break I returned to the flowers to paint them, creating the texture of the petals' surface with nail polish. Each petal was no wider than the nail brush as I made the fine film by ensuring the brush touched both sides of the wire simultaneously. It didn't always work the first time so I often had to do it a couple of times. I made a few of these wire flowers and gave them to my mother in a small bouquet. It was all I could manage for now.

Towards the end of May Iiro returned to LA for some meetings and though I missed him, I was glad for some alone time. By now I had been with Iiro for just over a year and even though I was grateful for his love, support and companionship, co-living was an adjustment that took some getting used to.

In the three years before we met I had become accustomed to being alone so I just wasn't used to having someone around constantly. It was a revelation to be with someone who shopped, cooked and spent quality time with César. I loved it and Iiro was my rock helping me through this difficult time. I had to get used to relying on someone again, not just doing it all on my own, and I wasn't very good at that.

Now I asked my artist friend Misha Frisch to make a locket necklace for me. I had bought several of his works over the years: a large chandelier made from shoe lasts, a tree made from old oxygen tanks and a bracelet made from a bike chain for an aquamarine stone. I loved the way he repurposed old things and turned them into something new and beautiful. I wanted to put the twins' pictures inside the locket and wear it close to my heart.

Grieving

Misha also has twins, both girls. He knew mine before he moved to Germany. He started crying when we talked on the phone about the necklace, and I felt powerless that I was unable to comfort him.

At the end of the month I flew to Italy for a family reunion, to mark the first birthday since our grandfather's death. I had to admit, I wasn't sure whether to go or not. My parents said it would be nice to see me, there was talk of this being 'good' for me and I knew it might be beneficial to get out of the house and out of Cape Town for a week.

I didn't know if I was strong enough for it all. I felt heavy, weary and vulnerable, as if carrying my grief around like a boulder. Since this was a memorial event and none of the other sisters were taking their children, I decided to leave César with his cousins for the trip. But I felt anxious leaving him behind and cried a lot on the plane waiting for take-off.

The two flights seemed to go on forever. It was the first time I was truly alone and I had too much time to think and dwell on events. Even with my family at Lago Como, it was difficult. I felt fragile and exhausted and trying to hide this from them probably didn't help. *This is a time to remember my grandfather*, I kept reminding myself. *It's not about the twins*.

There were no expectations on me but my family gently encouraged me to take part in things, which I probably needed because, without their pushing, I probably would have just sat on my bed. Though it was refreshing to be somewhere different, my thoughts were with César and the twins the whole time.

On Opa's birthday we took a boat tour around the lake

with my sisters, parents, my step grandmother Heidi, her son Timm and my aunt Sissi and Carolin. We were out for about two hours, during which I spent most of the time in tears. Heidi came and sat with me, and we talked a little. I had told her about what happened on the day the twins were killed. I didn't mind talking about it. I felt like my friends and family had the right to know but I only gave out the information if they asked. I was finding that it got easier every time I told it. She was horrified and told me how sorry she was.

At the end of the four day trip, I was relieved to be going home. While it had been nice to see my family and have a change of scenery, the whole event felt traumatic and so hard. I missed César so much, more than any other time in my life. I worried about him the whole time, thinking of what he must be feeling, if he was alright, if he was struggling. My family had been wonderful but my grief was so deep and overwhelming at times the whole trip had been a strain.

Everyday interactions now became fraught with difficult choices. I struggled with telling people that I had three children. I couldn't say I only had one child as it would feel like I was betraying the twins' memory by not acknowledging them. But then I couldn't qualify that by saying that two of my children were no longer alive. I had no desire to lob a bomb like that into a conversation with a stranger. Still, I couldn't deny their existence, or the fact that I would always be a mother of three. This was one of the things that made me fearful – not recognising them in some way.

In my diary I channelled this profound grief and confusion:

Grieving

My loss isolates me from others. I feel different, locked out, unreachable. The parents of the children at nursery with the twins still run around after their children, their days overflowing with activity: mealtimes, baths, walks in the park, playdates, bedtimes, early mornings... I don't do any of that anymore. I feel lost without them.

Those who know me ask how I am surviving. I'm not really. It sometimes just seems overwhelming, I want to find a hole to crawl inside. I go through the motions, so ingrained in me, for the benefit of César. The rest of the time I'm faking it. I suppose everyone has different ways of coping. It would be so easy if there were a proven way to heal from grief. I suppose the basic is the same for most people, and that is talking, but even that is not something everyone wants to do.

Sometimes it just seems so futile. I read, I go for walks, see my therapist, do yoga and occasionally, if I can, I use my hands creatively on one of my craft activities. I hope the combination of all of these will help me to recover.

Each day is more or less the same. It feels like I'm just trying to make it through, trying to help César by putting one foot in front of the other so I can get things done. Iiro and César keep me busy, and I try to do something creative every day. It seems I am calmer, more centred, and when I do think about them, it doesn't seem to be so bad.

I don't want Mario to win. I am fighting within myself not to become as pessimistic as he was, or to see the world as a dangerous place. If I took his outlook on life, I feel that he would have won in some way. I prefer to be optimistic, believe in the good in people, and be hurt or disappointed, rather than becoming anything close to what Mario represents for me. Yes, he shattered my heart. That will never mend, it is broken forever, but one day, far from now I will be better, even if I am broken. I will emerge stronger.

I am reading a book that Jeff's stepmother gave to me called "Healing after Loss". I think it helps me, but the problem I have with it is that it speaks a lot about adults who have lost husbands, wives or parents, but not about parents that have lost young children. I would like to find more books that deal with my kind of loss. I can't find any in the library here that resonate except one called "The Healing Code" by Dr Alexander Lloyd. It is helping. I have so many memories to help me but knowing that they will never experience anything again is quite unbearable.

The Memorial

*"I hope I can learn from my mistakes.
I hope that you felt loved by me.
I do feel loved by you, now and always."*

LETTER THIRTY

I drove along the wide boulevard of Dock Road with Table Mountain behind me and the V&A Waterfront straight ahead of me, deep in thought. It was early June and a week since I had received the text from Mario's brother Juan saying he was coming to Cape Town to see Mario and meet his lawyer. When he suggested we see each other I didn't hesitate.

Until now I'd had no contact with Mario's side of the family and I really didn't know what they thought. They had learned about the twins' death through the Spanish embassy here and since then nobody had reached out to me. Mario maintained that he didn't remember anything and on the first bail hearing his lawyers were unprepared and asked for a postponement. What did they make of it all? My statements were in English and though they had been translated into Spanish for Mario's family, they were not well written by the captain. I felt they needed to hear what really happened. And they needed to hear it directly from me.

I parked up outside the Dock House Hotel and walked through to the breakfast area where I spotted Juan at a table. Juan was two years older than Mario and I'd always found him to be a really nice man. He worked as a psychiatrist, had previously been through a divorce with his first wife, with whom he had two older children, and was now remarried with a son a year younger than César. He stood up when he saw me and greeted me warmly but I felt nervous as I sat down opposite him. We had always got along well but I had no idea how he would react to what I had to say. He offered his condolences and I accepted them solemnly. He seemed emotional but calm as he asked:

'What happened, Julia? We don't understand it. Please, tell me what happened…'

So I told him.

As the tears started flowing, the waiter offered to take us to a little private room so we could talk without the other guests seeing my distress. We took him up on this thoughtful gesture.

Juan remained still and unreadable throughout. It didn't look like anything I said was a surprise to him so I assumed he must have read my original statement. Perhaps he was trying to gauge if I was telling the truth? He accepted what I told him without disagreement or comment but he looked sad, and I could see it was taking a toll on him.

'How is Jan?' I asked. Jan was his little boy – he and César were very close in age and he had spent time with the twins during the holidays.

The Memorial

'I haven't told Jan yet,' he said sadly. 'He really loved his little cousins.'

What a tragedy this was, I thought. All these people were affected and would be for years to come. I asked how Juan's mother was coping.

'She's taking it badly,' he said. 'First my father, then the twins and now Mario is in prison here. It's too much for her.'

'Yes, I am sorry for her…'

It appeared to me that the family was standing by Mario, which I understood. Who else could Mario turn to for help? It didn't mean they supported his actions, even if they *believed* he had killed them. At this point I wasn't sure what they believed.

Until now, it had all happened so far away it must have seemed unreal and impossible to understand. At first there had been some idea floating around that the twins could have been murdered by an intruder but the security camera footage, showing nobody else entered the apartment – as well as the coroner's estimated time of death – had quickly eliminated this as a line of police enquiry. Was Mario – their brother, son, uncle – really a murderer? If it was my sister locked up for murdering her own children, I too would struggle to believe that she had done something so heinous. But I knew Mario did it. I was there. I just didn't understand how. How does a father kill his own children?

Juan had come to South Africa with a woman called Victoria who was both a friend of the family and their legal representative. While he was still in the hotel, making plans, she and I went outside. She took the opportunity while we were alone to ask, in a straightforward way, if I believed Mario was guilty of what the police said.

'Yes,' I replied simply.

'And do you think he acted knowingly and with intent?' she asked.

'Yes,' I repeated, looking her straight in the eye. She seemed to accept that.

César was at Vicky's house during our meeting and she suggested I invite Juan back for lunch afterwards. I thought this was a good idea as it would give César the chance to see and speak to his uncle. I still wanted them to have a relationship. Juan's three children were César's cousins after all and he still had a grandmother in Spain. I didn't want him to lose them all because of his father's actions.

Once we had finished talking, I asked Juan and his friends for lunch. Initially Juan did not want to come, but he arrived a little later with one of his friends. His other friend, Victoria, said she could not be there as she was a lawyer and the spokesperson for the family in Spain. I thought that was decent of her and told her I appreciated her gesture. She also made a strange comment. Although she didn't know Mario that well, she said she always saw him *con aires de grandeza*, that he thought himself better than anyone else. She nailed it perfectly, I thought, as I got back in my car. As it turned out, the lunch at Vicky's was nice and relaxed and we all sat down for pizzas together. It felt like the right thing to do and I was grateful for my sister's generosity and understanding.

Iiro, on the other hand, was not happy that I had met with Juan and seen him alone.

'It's irresponsible,' he insisted. 'You shouldn't have gone to a hotel by yourself.'

'There was no danger,' I replied. I thought he was over-reacting. In fact, Iiro and my family had been far more concerned about security since the twins' death than I was.

To my mind, the only dangerous person was now locked up in prison. To their thinking, Mario had made threats to me in the past and now, anything was possible. The only person who could testify to what he had done was me and in their eyes that made me a threat. If he wanted, he could hire someone to hurt me or try to scare me. So, to mollify my father, we hired a security guard to patrol the perimeter of the house and make sure nobody was there. Mario had told me previously that a friend of his was ex-KGB and Russian mafia. He had mentioned this person when I suggested he talk to someone about our divorce.

'If I tell anyone it will be my Russian friend,' he'd replied. 'But I wouldn't do that because then I'd have to work hard to hold him back so he wouldn't come and hurt you.'

By that time I didn't believe everything Mario told me and refused to take the threat seriously. The family felt it wasn't worth the risk.

We were planning a memorial in Spain in June and now I told Iiro I had invited Juan, his mother and the rest of Mario's family.

He shook his head: 'It's a bad idea. I don't understand why Juan would come, especially as he is paying for Mario's lawyer.'

'This isn't about Juan, me, Mario or any of us,' I replied.

'It's about the babies and their memorial service. But most importantly, it is about César. If César, in the end, does not want anything to do with the family, that's his choice. But I don't want to take the option away. They are his blood relatives.'

'Well, I won't be very warm towards Juan when I see him,' he said. 'I'll be on my guard, making sure he doesn't do anything untoward.'

'He's not going to do anything. What do you think he will do?'

I could understand this was difficult for Iiro but Juan was nothing like his brother. He was much more down to earth. This was a painful tragedy for his family as much as for ours and though he had natural loyalties towards his brother, it didn't make him any less broken-hearted for the loss of the twins. I wanted César to be in contact with his Spanish side of the family. I thought it would be good for him to see that even though he shared his father's DNA, they weren't all bad. I felt sorry that Iiro couldn't see things from my point of view but I accepted that he was struggling with it all too.

'Please understand, I have to trust my instincts on this,' I told Iiro. 'I have to do what I feel is right.'

Still, I was dreading having to go through another memorial again. It would be very hard to face all my friends and family. As much as I knew they would be there with unconditional love and support for me, talking to people about the twins still felt so painful and difficult.

In Palamos, we had 35 of our friends and family for dinner at our hotel the night before the memorial service. I was determined that it shouldn't be grim, like a wake, and wanted to celebrate their life, even though I didn't feel like being upbeat or entertaining. It felt like a long dinner and the effort of being out in public was wearing but I was pleased to be surrounded by friends and family. I sat next to my cousin Carlos who had lost his son Marco when he was three from leukaemia.

'When Marco died I made a conscious decision,' he said. 'I chose not to think of him and to try to forget. My wife Elena did the opposite. She always talks about him. All the time.'

It was interesting to hear their different ways of coping, though I didn't ask him more. He had just told me he wanted to forget so it would be wrong to pry. *I can't live like that. I will never try and forget my children*, I vowed. Just the opposite – it was one of my greatest fears that Maximo and Octavia would be forgotten.

The memorial, on June 18, was in Mas Del Vent, a lovely house we owned close to the beach which had a beautiful garden and a large pond. First we had lunch at Bell-Lloc, our family's country estate, and then went down to Mas Del Vent. It was a beautiful summer day, not too hot, just perfect. The garden looked lovely and felt so tranquil. Juan came with Marta, his wife, and his two older kids, Guillem and Aina, as well as his father-in-law, though Mario's mother did not come.

'She does not feel strong enough,' Juan explained.

I understood. César and I buried some of the twins' ashes at the base of the olive tree close to the pond where my grandfather and aunt were also buried. I was crying so much that I could barely see what I was doing and Iiro stepped in to help me.

Later, César went off to the pond in the garden on his own. A few people noticed, but Juan was the first to join him. I was pleased about that. César told me later that they talked about his toy guns that he had left at his father's house and asked Juan to send them to him. He also said that they talked about the twins. César needed to be able to share his feelings about his siblings with his family and though he was finding it easier to talk to me, he was still wary that any discussion about the twins would make me cry. And he hated to see me cry.

The day before we buried the ashes, Iiro said he needed to talk to me. We went and sat down on the outside sofa, where he cried for a while. I was shocked to see him so distressed.

'What is it?' I asked.

'It's the whole situation with Juan,' he said. 'I just don't think you appreciate how difficult and stressful this is for me. You know, I tried to bring it up a few days ago but you dismissed me and said we were not going to talk about it.'

I felt guilty for batting away his concerns.

'You don't seem to appreciate the seriousness of the situation,' he said.

It's true that I didn't know why he was so against Juan and perhaps I had been unwilling to hear his concerns until now.

'Go on,' I said. 'I'm listening now.'

'In the future, if Mario's family still support him, and they have contact with César, they might tell him something else and confuse him.'

The Memorial

I sat back and thought about this.

'I don't believe that would happen,' I said thoughtfully. 'But I can see you have a point.'

'Yes, maybe I do, maybe I don't. Ask someone. Talk to César's psychologist to see what she thinks. And speak to Gary, your psychologist. I'm trying to make sense of everything myself but I haven't talked to anyone about this, and have only been with you and your family.'

Now it struck me that Iiro had not been able to offload to anyone as he had not seen any of his close friends lately. He needed to be heard. I agreed to bring up his concerns with the psychologists and he said he felt much better after our talk.

We had a few relaxing days before flying to Mallorca to spend time on my father's yacht where we joined his crew competing in a regatta. For two days I enjoyed the movement of the boat and the sound of the waves as we raced towards the next buoy. It was an exciting change of pace and I found myself caught up in the action, able to throw myself into the intensity of the race.

Luckily, we didn't have to do too much beyond staying out of the way of the racing crew but it was thrilling to be aboard as they dashed about, adjusting our sails and position perfectly to propel the boat along at optimum speed.

We had a few days of excellent sailing and won the overall race and our class. It was an outstanding achievement and everyone was ecstatic. I found myself wearing a genuine smile for the first time in weeks, able to share the joy with the rest of the crew.

I felt lighter afterwards. I'd been able to disconnect from the pain, if only for a short while, and the sea air had blown away some of the cobwebs and replaced it with a new energy. I always liked the ocean. It seems to renew me somehow.

César didn't have too much fun onboard though and complained about not being allowed to use his iPad. His cousin Lola was also with us, and although they played together, César seemed to be a little on edge. Each day we'd board the boat in the harbour and then returned to the hotel at night to sleep. One night after dinner, we were making our way back to the hotel when César asked to buy sweets from a shop we were passing.

'Not now, César,' I frowned. 'It's nearly midnight.'

'I want to get sweets,' he said grumpily. It was late and he was very tired.

'It's too late for sweets, César,' I insisted.

'I WANT SWEETS!' he yelled, and then burst into tears. He was still just seven years old. I tried to calm him down and reason with him that he could have sweets tomorrow.

'I'm going on my iPad when we get back,' he huffed.

'César, it's bedtime when we get back. Not iPad time.'

He lost it, screaming and crying. I decided to ignore this outburst and keep walking. He walked behind us most of the way. When I looked back to check he was following, he had taken off his T-shirt and was sitting in the middle of the road.

'What are you doing?' I asked, mystified.

'I want to be a street kid so I'm staying here,' he said. I didn't know what to do. First, we tried to convince him to come with us but he wouldn't budge so I took his hand and literally dragged him to the hotel, kicking and screaming the whole way. Luckily, there was no one around to witness this horrible scene.

Once we got to the room he tried to escape. When he realised he couldn't, he crawled into the corner and cried. I sat down on the bed next to him and thought about what I should say. It seemed I took too long for him.

'When are you going to talk?' he asked.

'César, I don't understand your behaviour,' I replied. 'What's going on? Why did you do that tonight – take your shirt off and say you wanted to live on the streets?'

'What happens to me when something happens to you?' he said. 'If I'm already living on the streets I can have a new mom and I don't have to worry about losing you.'

Oh, César!

'You will never be alone,' I told him. 'If I weren't around you would have Vicky and Omi and Opa and Iiro. You have other family members that love you and want the best for you. But look, I won't go anywhere. I will do my best to stay with you as long as I can.'

Iiro also talked to him, but he gave César a bit of a guilt trip by pointing out what he was putting me through. I didn't feel this was helpful and told Iiro as much. Sometimes the most well-intentioned actions can actually do more harm than good. I told César how much we both loved him and left it at that.

I went to brush my teeth and get a remedy to help him calm down and relax. He drank it and got ready for bed. He slowly came over, gave us hugs and said he loved us. It had been a difficult evening but I was grateful that César had been able to express the fears and the anxieties which played on his mind. It was hardly surprising. He was still so young and the worst thing imaginable had happened to him. It was hard to comprehend how profoundly this would affect him.

After Mallorca, we flew to Ibiza for the rest of the summer holidays. On the plane, César played with a little girl sitting behind him. It broke my heart to see how good he was with small children, knowing that he had the experience, and now had no one to play with at home. I too missed having little ones at home.

Iiro and I had spoken about having a child before but I always said I wasn't ready. Now I thought about it again. I longed for another child but I was fearful that I'd be trying to replace Maximo and Octavia. And that would not be fair on the new baby. The age gap with César would also be significant. Was that a good thing or not? I didn't know. It certainly meant César would also have to wait a while until the baby was big enough to play.

We were in Ibiza for a week where I had time to read, swim and sunbathe on the boat which the crew had sailed to meet us. For several days we sailed around the beautiful island of Formentera, a wilder and less known Balearic island.

At about 11am on the July 6 I realised with a jolt that it was the three-month anniversary of the twins' death. It took me by surprise that this day could nearly have passed me by. I suppose because I was on holiday I was not sure what day it was but it seemed unthinkable that I almost forgot such a day. *How have three months passed already? It felt like it was only yesterday that I found them in their beds.*

Back in Cape Town I visited the jeweller who was making my heart pendant of the twins. Misha had sent his design to Harald, of Aurum Design, who got a bit of a shock when I started crying as he hadn't realised that I was the mother. I saw how the design was coming along and I loved it. It will be so beautiful and simple. I had also resolved to get a tattoo with the twin's names – that would be next.

It was Iiro's birthday on July 13 and that morning I sent him a short WhatsApp message when I woke up. As his birthday fell the day before César's I really didn't have time to do anything else. I was too busy organising César's big day and since Iiro was away in Helsinki, I hadn't yet bought him a present or written a card. Instead, I poured all my energy into making César's day as good as it could possibly be.

This was César's eighth birthday and his first without the twins. I worried that it would be raining and cold on the day since the summer months are winter in South Africa and he would be upset if his laser gun party had to be postponed because of the rain. He was already going to miss the twins, he told me as much the day before, so I hoped that a party would take his mind off them and allow him to enjoy himself. Thankfully, it turned out to be a lovely day. In the morning, we did the usual birthday rituals with the cake and presents, which César enjoyed. It helped that he had no school that day so we didn't need to rush off afterwards.

As for me, I struggled all day long. My thoughts kept returning to the twins and how they would never enjoy another birthday. Next month they would have turned four but the day would be no celebration, just a painful reminder of their absence. I tried not to think about it. I tried my hardest to bury those thoughts and feelings of despair in order to give César a happy mother for his special day.

I had organised the party in a park close to home and invited his friends. Later we enjoyed drinks, snacks and the cake there. I was relieved that it gone as well as I could have hoped but that night, after César was in bed, I let the sadness envelop me. My babies would never have a birthday again.

Meanwhile, Iiro was in Finland with his parents. His older brother had died some years before but I guess being with his family reminded him of their own loss. This was another year celebrating without his brother. The next day Iiro seemed distant on the phone.

'What's wrong?' I asked.

'I don't know… it was my birthday two days ago and all I got from you was a WhatsApp message. I have friends on the other side of the world who put in more effort… singing to me with the whole family.'

I was stung.

'Iiro… I've been going through my own issues here, you know.'

'I know, I know… but it was my *birthday*. I've been here for you. I guess I just needed a bit of appreciation.'

'I'm sorry I can't be there for you. I'm thinking more of César and what will not happen next month. There will be no birthday in August this year. I'm sorry, Iiro, I'm sorry I can't be what you need me to be right now.'

The Memorial

After I put the phone down, I wondered if I was strong enough to take care of a relationship. Iiro wasn't happy but there was very little I felt I could do about it. Right now, it was all I could manage just to be there for César. He was a little boy. Iiro was a grown man. *Either it works or it doesn't. I don't have the energy to put into it at the moment.*

Iiro and I went through a rough couple of days. It was the first time that a rift had opened up between us and I felt bad about it all. He had needs of his own and I had to recognise that. Eventually he called and apologised.

'I'm sorry, Julia. I've just been very down and depressed the past week or so. My birthday also brings up difficult things for me. Losing my brother to cancer so young was hard. But I don't have a right to take out my feelings on you. I know the timing was bad and I couldn't expect it of you at that moment.'

'I understand,' I replied. 'It's fine. I'm sorry you've been through this alone.'

Although this difficult time between us was soon over, it gave me a moment's respite from my own grief. I realised that I had been locked in a bubble for the past few months. I had to see outside my own pain and be aware that other people were going through their own suffering. This wasn't only happening to César, Iiro and me, but to family and friends.

A friend mentioned that they knew someone from Durban who had heard the story on the news and had been deeply traumatised by it.

That blew my mind.

It never occurred to me that their deaths might affect

strangers. I have been too wrapped up in thinking about César and not much else. I need to be more aware that everyone has their baggage to carry. Each person sees things through lenses that get shaped by their experiences. Rightly or wrongly, these are their perceptions.

My viewpoint was changing, I was just starting to realise how unaware I had been. A quote from Martha Whitmore Hickman's *Healing After Loss* now returned to my mind: 'Think about where you are suffering in your life and then think about all the other people who are going through a similar situation. This perhaps is quite literally the birth of compassion, which means suffering within.'

It was time to look outside myself.

When Iiro returned to Cape Town I told him that I felt it was the right time to try for a baby – the sooner the better. He was over the moon. Though he was great with César I knew he wanted a child of his own. Now I made an appointment to take the Mirena IUD out. I was nervous but knew this was normal. At least I had a partner who was as committed to this new path as I was and, when the time came, we would bring up our child together. Nothing was guaranteed in this life. Iiro and I could break up tomorrow, another tragedy could strike, but I couldn't let that stop me.

One of the things I had said in the beginning to Iiro when we discussed children was that I didn't want to bring up another child on my own. But that didn't matter to me now. I knew I could do it if I had to, and it felt more important to have another child. The twins were taken so early, I felt like I had unfinished business.

The Memorial

Although you never stop being a mother, or father, I needed the opportunity to try again. There was never any question of replacing the children – that was not my intention – but I was aware that having a baby would help me with my healing. And since I was sure this would be my last child, I was certain I would enjoy motherhood all the more.

Disconnected

*"I know that my life has to go on for César's sake
and mine, but the guilt is sometimes
too much at the moment."*

LETTER FORTY-THREE

I found out from Juan Smuts in July that the bail hearing
was postponed for a second time. He told me that Mario's
lawyer, William Booth, had only just heard some of the evidence and seemed surprised by much of it, as Mario claimed
not to remember what happened on the day. Booth needed
more time to look into the case. Vicky, who went to see the
proceedings, said Booth appeared to talk a lot with no exact
point. He made no request to refer the accused for psychi-
atric evaluation, and Mario was ordered to be retained at
Pollsmoor prison medical section.

The state's lawyers objected to bail as they argued that
Mario was a flight risk and could be a danger to me as well
as his surviving son. I was only involved insofar as I was a
witness for the State's case and mother of the victims. I had
no say in the case itself – it was the state versus Mario –
but Juan kept me fully informed of what was going on and

the police too were good at keeping me updated with developments. The process seemed unbearably long and drawn out but I consoled myself with the thought that as long as they conducted their enquiries thoroughly then they should get the right result. Sometimes I felt an urge to go to the hearings as I was curious to know what I would feel when I saw Mario again. I held no anger for him, which I thought was strange.

Now the prosecutor asked me to print any relevant emails between Mario and me. There were thousands but I set about diligently going about this task, searching for emails that might be indicative of Mario's behaviour and state of mind. It took me forever as I had to read them all to see if they were relevant before printing. It was a very unwelcome trip down memory lane which didn't help my anxiety or self-doubt. Now I read in those emails all the hatred and venom that Mario had for me. I think at the time I tried hard to see beyond his anger, to put it to one side for the sake of peace and stability, but I read them now with fresh eyes. *Had I done the right things during the divorce? Did I push him so far that he felt he had to kill the babies? Should I have been more understanding?*

I knew in my logical mind that he was responsible for his actions but it didn't help going over things like this, thinking of what I could or should have done. I recalled that at the time, I felt like I was giving all I could, but maybe, just maybe I could have done more to prevent him becoming so angry. Would it have helped? How could I have known? All these questions went round in my mind and I would never know the answers. Sometimes I was tempted to go see Mario, but I knew that he would never answer my questions, if he even agreed to see me. I did not want him to see me broken. I didn't want to give him that gratification.

Meanwhile, I had an alienating sense of feeling disconnected from the world, from my own feelings. Maybe I wasn't facing my grief, I wasn't sure, but I felt like I was missing something, the bigger picture. I sought out answers in books, hoping to find the key to unlocking this part of me, something that would help me move forward and remind me to live, not just to survive. I found words that spoke to me, thoughts from others that helped me feel less alone on this vast sea of grief – and clung to them like life rafts.

'Some things cannot be fixed, they can only be carried,' wrote Megan Devine in her book *It's OK That You're Not OK*. And Sheryl Sandberg in her book *Option B* about losing her husband: 'Let me not die while I am still alive.'

I searched the shelves at the library for books by parents grieving the loss of a child but couldn't find any. Maybe I was looking in the wrong place. I wrote in my diary:

My heart feels small and empty. To live, there has to be meaning and joy. I find it through César and Iiro, but I need something more, and that is difficult. There always seems to be something holding me back. I don't know if it's the guilt for moving forward or just a blanket of sadness that sits on me and weighs me down. Gary made a comment that stuck with me: 'Grief is the love that you feel for the person who is no longer with you, which now has nowhere to go.' I think this is true.

Disconnected

There were endless delays in getting all the various medical reports back. It appeared there was a backlog and they did not have the facilities to do the analysis in Cape Town so they had to be sent off to labs in different parts of the country. Juan Smuts called me after having seen part of the autopsy report. He said that the twins had been smothered. We always suspected it, but having it confirmed made it seem more real somehow. And brought back the pain and shock of finding them.

At night I lay awake, wondering what they had gone through. *Did they know? Were they scared? Did they ask, or wonder, where I was? Why I wasn't there to help them?* My mind reached back into the past to try to untangle the series of choices that had led to this unfathomable action. I edged myself along the timeline of events, like winding in a ball of wool, my mind working at the knots, trying to understand. If I couldn't undo what he had done, at least I could unravel the truth. But no matter how I tried to look at things, it all led back to the same unbearable state of affairs. *My children are dead...* and the despair descended quickly. Would this feeling of being pulled down into the pit of a deep dark well never leave me?

Information came in dribs and drabs from Juan Smuts and Brian Oosthuizen, the police warrant officer in charge of the case. We were told that Mario had apparently arranged with a friend to pick him up from the airport in Spain but a few days before he was due to fly back, he told him not to come as he had changed his plans and was flying somewhere else. It looked like he had planned to escape and disappear.

Then the toxicology reports came back. It appeared that Mario had given the twins something before he suffocated them as there were no signs of a struggle. That was a small blessing. Sam said that Maximo and Octavia had received a pink drink in the morning and that they did not remember anything after that.

I had quite a few lengthy meetings with Brian about my upcoming court appearance. He talked me through the sort of questions I would likely be asked and how Booth would act towards me once I was in the witness box. He also asked me to go over my statement and flesh it out more. I had made the original statement the day after the murder, as I thought it best to do it when the memories were fresh, and to get it over and done with. But because it was a very long and tiring experience, I realised that it sounded robotic. So I added some detail to my previous statement and that brought me to tears.

The next day I decided that the statement was messy and wrote down events from scratch as I remembered them. That got me going again, and I let myself sob deeply. It was always surprising how that seemed to help. I still had the deep despair but felt like some of the weight had lifted.

The new bail hearing was postponed to September and I wanted to go, to ensure that Mario was not granted bail. The only thing that concerned me was the knowledge that there would be media there. I had no desire to face the press but if my presence in court helped to ensure that Mario did not get bail, they wouldn't stop me. I also wanted to see the lawyer who was defending Mario – William Booth.

Disconnected

I thought a lot about what I would say when I was finally called on to testify.

It was finally confirmed in August 2017 that Mario had given Maximo and Octavia medicine containing valproic acid, usually given to people with epilepsy, to prevent migraines or to treat bipolar disorder. It made the person sleepy. This explained why there were no signs of a struggle.

The police said Mario had not purchased the medicine in South Africa as you needed a doctor's prescription to get it in this country and he didn't visit a doctor in the time he was here. That meant he had bought it before the trip and got rid of the bottle at some point before his arrest. It wasn't found either in the apartment or the car when he was apprehended.

There was CCTV evidence from the apartment that showed he had walked out of the compound for a short while alone before I arrived on the day of the murders and there was some speculation that he could have disposed of the medicine container then.

It didn't matter.

The toxicology evidence was sufficient to prove premeditated murder, for which Mario could get 25 years if found guilty. It was a major breakthrough and led to the charges of murder being laid against Mario.

It saddened me to be proven that Mario had planned this. That he was able to think of the death of his own children by his own hand for weeks, if not months in advance. The hate he had to feel for me to be able to do this to them was heartbreaking and guilt swept through me as I realised the part I had played in it.

The bail hearing finally took place in September 2017 and I decided not to go in the end as I would not be called as a witness and I didn't know how it would affect me to see Mario.

Thankfully, bail was denied. That was a relief. I don't know how I would have felt if Mario had been freed. Certainly there appeared to be evidence that he was going to attempt to flee the country after the twins' murder. When he was first arrested, the police had found passports in the flat – a French and South African passport with unknown names and the pictures didn't match. Was there another woman involved? Was he planning to put his picture in the passport to make an escape? If that had been his plan, why didn't he have them on him when he fled? A lot of things didn't seem to make sense to me but at least the judge had been persuaded that Mario was a flight risk.

The case dragged on. For a long time there was talk of a negotiated settlement where Mario would make a plea in order to secure a reduced sentence. But the case against him was very strong and it appeared the defence was not willing to make appropriate concessions. He had been charged with two counts of murder, two counts of assault, kidnapping, theft and theft of a motor vehicle. Though he maintained he didn't remember anything about that day, he did claim that the car incident was caused when the sun blinded his vision. But after a reconstruction it was established that the sun was in fact behind him when he was driving.

I would have been happy to have been spared the trauma

of going to trial but I couldn't trade that for Mario escaping justice. To my mind he had to pay the price for snatching those two young lives, so full of promise, so full of potential. I felt he must at least serve 20 years in prison and through my lawyer, communicated this to the state's prosecutor.

There were over 50 witnesses lined up to take the stand but all attempts to come to an agreement ended without success. The trial was ordered to go ahead, with three weeks court time set aside in March 2018.

Unfortunately there were problems finding suitable translators for Mario. Although he spoke some English, it wasn't strong enough to allow him to understand everything that was said in court so he needed a highly-skilled Spanish translator. According to Booth, Spanish translators were not paid an adequate daily rate to secure these services for the court proceedings. It was very frustrating that time dragged on without any resolution. I was desperate for Mario to pay for his crimes. It was so important to me that he take responsibility for all the pain he had caused and the waiting felt interminable.

In my diary I wrote:

How much it still hurts. My broken heart will always be broken, that will never change. I hope that the judge sees the pain Mario has caused and give him the maximum time in prison. I worry that Mario will see that he has succeeded in hurting me, or maybe he will think that he has not done enough and will try to do some more harm.

I never felt hate towards him. I still do not. It is something I sometimes wondered about as it did not seem normal. *I should hate him. Did this lack of hate show that I was detached? I was not feeling deeply enough?* But in the end all I find is sadness. Sadness that he was capable of something like this, sadness for him feeling like he needed to do this to hurt me and deep despair that I, without realising what he was capable of, had pushed him so deep into a corner that he did not see another way out.

Narcissist

*"My anxiety isn't getting any better. I had to force
my breathing, but it made the anxiety worse.
I went to see a GP who gave me some medication
to make it much more manageable."*

LETTER FORTY-FOUR

Regardless of the progress of the criminal case against Mario, I had to try to come to terms with the incomprehensible deaths of my two children. I had to try to understand what had led Mario to commit such an inhuman act – and I had to try to find a way to live with the consequences.

This would be the hardest task. Nobody wants to imagine what they would do if their children were taken away from them young, nobody should. And yet, here I found myself, in an alternative reality to the one I had thought would persist. *How do I live with the absence of my children? How do I quieten the despair inside me enough to live beyond merely existing?*

I read many books but one in particular spoke to me – *The Book of Forgiving* by Desmond and Mpho Tutu. It not only helped me to understand the steps I needed to take to forgive but also told the story of the American parents of scholar

Precious Scars

Amy Biehl, killed in a racially motivated attack in Cape Town while working as an anti-Apartheid activist in South Africa.

Amy's parents supported amnesty for her killers and hired two of them to work for the Amy Biehl Foundation offering programmes for youngsters in marginalised communities. I couldn't imagine being able to work with the killer of my child, but their strength and courage gave me hope. Just knowing that there were people out there who could do that helped me to see a way through. Redemption was possible.

Some people took the wrong path, but with the right help and support they could find their way back on track. That these parents could forgive their daughter's killers so fully as to embrace them and offer them an olive branch illuminated a path towards healing that I had not seen before.

'Without forgiveness, we remain tethered to the person who harmed us. We are bound with chains of bitterness, tied together, trapped,' I read in the book. It inspired me to start looking for a place for forgiveness in my heart.

The book also helped me understand Mario better. At least I thought it did. I could be totally off base, but I thought he was locked in a perpetual cycle of revenge. He felt so hurt and his ego so bruised that he needed to give back in kind. He did not mourn our relationship and did not come to terms with the ending of it. He saw me as someone preventing him from spending time with his kids and cutting him off from a certain kind of lifestyle that he was not ready to lose.

I never realised that the man I married and the father of my children was a narcissist. Mario had airs of grandeur, and nothing was ever his fault. He had the drive to become successful, but he was envious of what others had, believing that he lacked these characteristics. I saw these traits separately but never put them together. I was told by different people that he was a narcissist, but he was never diagnosed as one.

It was Sam, my counsellor, who had first used the word 'narcissist' with me during the divorce. She was also a trained psychologist and when I told her about some of the ways he had reacted she had replied: 'He is sounding more and more like a narcissist.'

It got me thinking and I went away and looked up Narcissistic Personality Disorder (NPD). When I saw the top traits it certainly seemed to fit Mario's personality. He wanted to be seen as important and having means. I recalled the fixation he'd had of employing a butler and a nanny and having 'staff'. Also, the consulate job. For him, it was all about seeming important and having status. He was obsessed with having consulate plates so that he could go through security and double park anywhere without getting a fine. Mario was enamoured with the idea of being special, getting special treatment, enjoying exemptions, being a VIP. He had a sense of being more entitled than others and that's why I thought Juan's friend had hit the nail on the head when she said he had 'airs of grandeur'.

I could now see that being with me had fed into this idea he had of himself as a man of special importance. I recalled the time, not long after we had married, when he wanted to open an account with a very exclusive bank. I didn't know what the requirements were to get an account at this bank but he used my family name to do it. I was in the meeting with him when he turned to the bank manager and said: 'Yes, because she is Julia Engelhorn, daughter of Kurt.' I gave him a funny look, thinking to myself: *Who gives you the right to use my name like this?* But then I ignored it afterwards, never mentioning it to him.

He was a dentist but he saw himself in another role, that of an investor, which is how he had ended up with one million euros out of our family trust. The problem was he had no experience of investing and was secretive about what he was up to. We'll never know where all that money went and the debt remains on me. He came from an ordinary family but ordinary things were beneath him. He was too superior to go to a supermarket, to change a nappy or to fly economy class.

We once took a trip to Madrid to see friends of his and because the flight was less than an hour from Barcelona I organised some cheap tickets. We were squeezed into the middle seats at the back of the plane and he wasn't happy. It was a stopover on a flight to South America so we got out and most people stayed in. He was squashed between two people and complained endlessly about it. By then he was used to a certain standard of travel, flying either business or first class.

I think he assumed I would never divorce him and therefore he would be set for life. He never paid a mortgage, utility bill or for any of the help that we had at home. His money was all his own, and though he made a good living for himself when we first met, by the end of our relationship he didn't work and claimed not to have a steady income of his own.

Narcissist

I was his passport to the better life he always thought he deserved. When I decided that our relationship was over he interpreted it as me snatching all that away from him. I failed to take account of the enormous impact this would have on his state of mind.

Like many narcissists, Mario didn't appear to see people as having intrinsic value. They were only of worth insofar as they could further his aims and interests. He seemed to have no real interest in friends, family or their feelings. I recalled how, when we made friends with other couples, it would start off very intense. He would make lots of arrangements with the husband, I would see the woman on my own, taking time to build the relationship. But then he would inevitably find something wrong with the man. They would fall out and he would insist I stop socialising with the wife too.

It was frustrating that my friendships were curtailed because of his difficulties, but over time I came to notice that he seemed unable to really maintain any friendships, constantly demanding that those people respect him, admire him, treat him the way he expected to be treated. It was the same with my family. At first he had charmed everyone, making great efforts to cosy up to my parents and sisters. But then, once we were married, he dropped the pretence and stopped coming to any family gatherings. He just wasn't interested in anyone else and I didn't see that for a very, very long time. Mario had an inflated ego and needed everyone around him to treat him as the special, important person he felt he was.

There was nobody he saw regularly and he could only

maintain a friendship as long as there wasn't much contact – once a year, at most. He simply had no desire or ability to keep up the relationship, no real interest in that person or their life. 'Why should I bother if he doesn't do it?' he complained. 'Why should I be the first one to call?' It never occurred to him to do anything simply because that person was a friend, a person he liked. He didn't seem interested in them.

Before we divorced he told me that if his parents asked after him I should confirm he had been in South Africa, even when he wasn't. He lied to them frequently about his whereabouts because he didn't want to go and see them. He thought he was better than everyone else and nobody was worth the effort. He did, however, enjoy all the trappings and the lifestyle which being with me afforded him.

And he was never in the wrong.

With the dental practice, for example, if something went awry it was always the nurse's fault. Or the person who had supplied the products. The practice took a while to take off and it was pretty clear that was because it wasn't in a good location. But he couldn't accept that he had chosen a difficult place to start the business. He never attempted to understand why things fell apart. It was always someone else's fault. I never once heard him reflect that he could have done something better. At least that's what it seemed like to me. The impression I got from how he acted. But of course I could be wrong, as I was wrong about so many things.

That was why divorcing him was the worst thing I could have done. It couldn't possibly be his fault. He had done nothing wrong. I had simply decided, vindictively, in his mind, to take away everything he felt he deserved. And in the process he lost control. He wanted to take some of that back and make me pay for his pain. That was why he had lied about being ill. It was a way of maintaining some control over my emotions and behaviour. At the very least it got me to hold off telling anyone about the divorce for many months, though I would have done that anyway in the interests of trying to work out an amicable arrangement.

I have subsequently learned that narcissists frequently lie about their own health to manipulate others. At the time I really didn't see the point but now I think about it, he used it to get his way and perhaps he hoped if I believed he was that ill I wouldn't divorce him at all. In truth, he had been very successful in manipulating me throughout our relationship and while others saw through his deceit, I always gave him the benefit of the doubt. I saw the Mario he wanted me to see, not the real man, even to the point of defending him to my family when he refused to spend Christmas with us! He really did have me fooled.

In the beginning there was love. I can't be sure when that changed. Maybe when we moved to South Africa and we were not together? Or maybe it was before then? Maybe I felt the change in the relationship because he had changed and blamed myself and how I had changed. It's impossible to figure out now.

So it must have come as a huge shock when I stopped playing his game. To his mind the rejection was unwarranted and unfair. It wounded his precious ego and to make me pay he became mean and spiteful, attempting to inflict the maximum amount of pain for the ignominy of putting him through a divorce. There couldn't possibly be a reason for rejecting him, of course. I had behaved badly and for that I must be punished. The high-conflict split should have been more of a warning, but I would never have believed that he was capable of doing what he did.

Even if he knew that he was a narcissist, he would not have seen it as negative, as narcissists perceive their characteristics to be highly beneficial to them. I have since learned that a high percentage of murderers are narcissists. It makes sense. You would have to imagine that the person's life you are taking has no intrinsic value in order to feel empowered enough to snuff it out.

I couldn't change him, but now, knowing the person he was, I felt I might have worked harder to understand him and perhaps if I had communicated better and I had said what was bothering me the divorce would not have come as such a shock. He genuinely had no idea I was unhappy and that had always struck me as strange. When I talked to him about the breakdown in our marriage, I had blamed myself, telling him I had changed after César's birth. But really I should have made him take responsibility for the decisions he made that led to the end of the marriage.

Not everyone changes when they have children but there is a balance to be struck between our needs and the needs of the little ones we have brought into this world. A shared vision of parenthood definitely helps to contribute to a happy relationship. It is not the only ingredient, but an important one since children take up most of our time and love. In the end, I had let him go without making this clear and perhaps that was my error.

It had allowed him to think of himself as the victim the entire time, being made to suffer the indignities of a divorce through absolutely no fault of his own. Losing his home, losing his children, losing access to the lifestyle he had assumed would always be there. And his anger grew and grew. Of course, he was responsible for his actions. Murder is never the answer. But I had my part in it, and for that, I sought forgiveness. Not from Mario, but from myself. I needed to forgive myself.

My forgiveness could not come with strings attached. I was not doing it for Mario, but for myself and César. I would always grieve for Maximo and Octavia. Grief was a reminder of the depth of my love. It ached and was unbearable at times, but I embraced it as a reminder of the beauty of that love that was now lost.

But I didn't want the death of my twins to perpetuate more revenge and hate. César needed to see that there was a better and different option. This was very important to me. I hoped he would grow up to understand that. He might not be ready to forgive now, he might never be, but at least he could see that it was possible, and that I would be there to help him, if and when he needed it.

I read more. *The Book of Forgiving* by Desmond and Mpho Tutu was so good I couldn't put it down. It seemed to send vibrations through me when I read it. I spent my free time doing the exercises it recommended to begin the journey of forgiving. I wrote down thoughts in the margins of the book, mostly questions, but it seemed that as soon as I wrote them down, I had an answer. It also helped me see that forgiving Mario was just one step, a big one, of many that I would have to take. I learnt that we forgive not only the big things but also the smaller mundane things, like the guy who cuts you off while driving. Forgiving was something I needed to practice every day and the book suggested praying for a person's well-being. When I read that I recoiled. I could not pray for Mario.

It took me a while to come to terms with it, but when I heard the same suggestion in an audio book I decided to give it a try, by starting with other people and situations. I realised that I benefited from this and it gave me a release from some anxiety. It didn't matter that I wasn't religious. I wasn't praying to a God as such. I was just holding that person in my heart for a moment and wishing them the best. The trouble was remembering to do it. I wondered if I should put post-its up everywhere, reminding me to forgive. *Then it will become a habit*, I thought. *Then Iiro will think I have gone off the rails!*

It helped to look at the bigger picture. Not every action was a personal attack directed at me. Most of the time, people are just not aware, they're angry at someone else, and more likely at themselves. We are all very hard on ourselves. We have to give ourselves a break.

It was hard for me to admit that I had, unknowingly of course, played a part in what happened. My negativity was part of it. Like the saying: 'Energy goes where attention goes.' I did not know what I know now. I was not as aware. Knowing this did not help with the guilt.

Forgiving Mario was an important part of helping me to accept the reality that the past couldn't be changed. And it took me by surprise that it was relatively easy to forgive him. He had acted on his demons, and I had added to them. Forgiving myself was not so easy. How odd – that I found it so much easier to forgive Mario than to forgive myself. *Why was that? Did I set my bar so high? Why was I so hard on myself? Did that mean I was harder than necessary on others?* It came down to the expectations I had of myself, even of others. Today, still, I carry the guilt. I don't know if it will ever leave me.

And what about justice? At first, I had worried that in forgiving Mario I would have to drop the expectation that he should pay for his crimes, but the more I read, the better I understood that this was not the case. One quote from *The Book of Forgiving* affected me very deeply: 'Forgiveness does not subvert justice – it creates space for justice to be enacted with purity of purpose that does not include revenge.'

Justice, not revenge. This was what I sought and now, the idea of a letter, as the book suggested, started to sound like an excellent idea. I decided to write to Mario, and maybe even read it out in court so I could be sure he heard what I had to say. If I gave it to him he might tear it up and never read it. But before I did anything, I would have to show the letter to Iiro and my family. Juan Smuts also had to give the OK, to make sure I wasn't saying anything that could hurt the case.

It took a couple of weeks as I kept going back to my letter

to make sure that I was happy with it. But the act of writing it was perhaps the greatest part of my work in forgiving Mario, forgiving myself and allowing myself to start to heal.

I wrote:

Dear Mario,

In the beginning we had a great relationship. You gave me three beautiful children, and although I was only able to keep two of them for a short while, I do not regret a moment of it.

I am deeply sorry that I hurt you so, and that my actions led you to believe that you needed to exact revenge on me. You were a great father to César, and I believe, that due to the divorce, you could not form the same connection to Maximo and Octavia. I believe that is why you decided to kill them and spare César. I am deeply grateful for that too. Having César has helped me to be strong for him, and to slowly and painfully move forward.

I am sorry that their lives meant so little to you, and that hurting me, to make me suffer and pay for my actions, was more important. I take responsibility for my part, for asking for the divorce in the way I did, for not handling the situation better, and for not seeing your point of view in this nightmare.

Your actions have left two big holes in my heart that will never heal. The grief is sometimes unbearable. You are no monster, as calling you that would take away the responsibility of your actions. You are just a man who believed that killing your children to make me suffer was worth the sacrifice.

Your actions have far-reaching consequences, not only for César and myself and my family, but for yours as well. They have to live not only with what their son and brother has done, but they will also have to grieve for the grandson, granddaughter, nephew and niece that you have robbed them of. Friends have been affected on both sides. And even strangers to you and me.

César has suffered dramatically. He misses being a big brother, and often feels responsible for not protecting his little siblings. That's what you have left him with. He has also lost his father and has to live with what you have done. He also has to live with guilt and pain. It is a difficult thing for a seven-year-old to wrap his mind around.

I forgive you. I do this not for you, but for myself, and most importantly for César. This does not come with any strings attached. I do not need you to forgive me or accept my forgiveness, or even believe me. This will not lessen my grief, and it does not mean that I do not seek justice for what you have done. There are consequences to the actions you have decided to take, and those need to be faced.

I hope you find some peace.

Julia

Found Dead

*"I have been writing less and less as I have not felt
the need. Although I was never very eloquent, it was
beneficial in the beginning to write down what I felt."*

LETTER FORTY-SIX

Iiro and the family were happy with the letter, but the lawyers
wanted me to wait until the trial was over and Mario convicted before giving it to him. They were worried that it could
be misunderstood and seen as a confession for having taken
part in the crime. I suppose their job was to look after me. I
anticipated giving it to Mario. It did not matter if I could not
read it out in court, just the act of writing the letter had been
a big step forward and I imagined it might help him to open
up to us one day. Maybe it would help César too.

After much toing and froing the trial date was finally set
for April 2019, exactly two years after the twins' death. The
lawyers were confident. We had a strong case, they said,
and even his lawyers conceded that Mario's behaviour had
been difficult, erratic and untrustworthy in the run-up to the
murders.

On January 14, 2019, I got a call from Juan Smuts to tell

me that Mario had been found dead in his prison cell. It was a very quick call as he had no further information apart from telling me that Mario had died.

He told me something along these lines: 'Hello Julia. I am just calling to let you know that I just received a call from Pollsmore prison. They found Mario dead in his cell this morning.'

I asked him how he had died but he was not able to give me any further details as the prison had not given him any. They were very tight-lipped about it as it was not good for them that an inmate was found dead.

It was a shock and at first I was not sure how to feel. I was not relieved as he had now escaped his punishment. I knew the trial would have been a terrible ordeal but at least at the end we would have had a result. He would have to face the consequences of his actions. But in taking his own life he had evaded that.

Maybe he wanted to control the narrative, but I think maybe he could not face a minimum of 25 years in a South African prison. Maybe he felt guilty for what he had done.

I was also overwhelmed with sadness, mostly for César, who had now lost his father, but also for Mario's family. I asked Juan if Mario had left behind any letter for César, and when he told me no, I was angry. He could have written something to César, a goodbye, an 'I love you'. Anything!

César was heading out of the house with Iiro, and I thought it best to tell him immediately about his father. Perhaps I should have taken time to do it with more consideration, but I didn't want him to hear it from someone else and, since I always told him everything straight away, keeping something from him, even only for a short time, felt wrong.

'I just got a call from my lawyer and he says they found your father – he had died in his bed,' I said slowly and steadily. 'He has taken his own life.'

César was silent, unsure it seemed how to react.

'Okay,' he said finally.

We sat together for a while, exchanging few words, but I could see he too was struggling to make sense of the news. He needed time to process what I'd told him and sort out his feelings. In that regard he was very like me.

Later that same day he came back with questions and though I did my best, I didn't have many answers myself.

'Was there a letter for me?' he asked.

'No.'

'What about a will? Did he leave anything behind for me?'

As far as I was aware there was no will but I promised I would look into it for César. He was, after all, Mario's only surviving child and whatever was left should go to him. The problem was that Mario never put anything in his name. In his constant quest to avoid paying taxes he had died without anything in his estate. And I assume that any money he had set aside was already spent on lawyers' fees, which is why his brother had asked me about money.

'How did it happen?' he asked.

'I think he took pills,' I said. 'But we are waiting for the results of a post-mortem to find out exactly what he took.'

I felt so sorry for him. My son was still so young and now he was in mourning for a murderous father who had decided to take his own life. It would have been hard for an adult to navigate this emotional minefield, let alone a child of nine. He loved his father, and I think that he would have liked to have seen him sometime in the future. Now it would never happen. It upset him that Mario had not left anything for him, not even a letter.

Fortunately, I still had photographs and some of Mario's things for César which I gave to him. And there is a classic car which belonged to Mario that I have kept for César if he still wants it in years to come. I couldn't blame my son for wanting something from his father. Mario was not evil. At some stage in my life, I had loved him and wanted to share my life with him. He had been a good father to César and the pair were once very close. César hated his father for what he had done but he was still the same father he had loved all his life, so those warm feelings were still there.

To this day he struggles to hold those two seemingly contradictory positions in his heart, and perhaps he will continue to struggle for years to come. It must be so hard for him. Mario was a very flawed human who made bad choices and though one can imagine how things could have been very different, they weren't and nothing can diminish the cruelty of what he did to César's siblings.

It took a long time to get any real answers about the suicide. It turned out that he had been hoarding painkiller medicine over a long period. And they had no clue. When Juan told me that he had committed suicide by taking an overdose of pills, I had an image of him lying on his back, looking as if he was asleep. But this was not how it happened. Mario had taken steps to avoid being discovered, placing a sponge in the peephole the guards use to check on prisoners.

When the prison guard finally found him, he was sitting on his lower bunk in his shorts, T-shirt and flip flops, slumped over and face down on the mattress. Pills were everywhere, spilling from his mouth and lying around him on the bed. I don't know how he was able to hoard such a large amount without it being discovered. He had complained about kidney stone pain ever since I knew him. Throughout this time in prison he had received medicine for this pain. Either he had lied about the pain to get the pills, or he suffered with the pain and did not take them. If that was the case, 20 months was a long time to suffer.

It surprised me that he decided to kill himself. I never thought that a narcissist would be able to do that. I found an article that said that narcissists who suffered from depression were more likely to commit suicide (Heisel et al, 2007). It seems that because their self-esteem is fragile, killing themselves is a reaction to a perceived narcissistic injury (Perry, 1990). But there are others that dispute this, saying they crave power and attention and have a deep fear of death. What was his motivation?

At the time of his death the police had evidence that he planned to murder his children even before arriving in South Africa so did he realise that he was likely to be found guilty at trial and imprisoned for a very long time? Was the prospect of a lifetime in Pollsmoor prison unbearable? Or was he determined not to suffer the indignity of being found guilty of murder? I guess in the end, whatever his motivation, it didn't matter. For Mario there was just one last thing he had control over, his own life, and whatever suffering he had caused to others he was not prepared to let anyone act as arbiter of his fate.

With Mario gone I decided to contact two of the people who had helped me on the day of the murders. I had planned to contact them anyway once the trial was over but now there was no reason not to do it straightaway. First, I returned to the parking attendant who had told me I should remember my licence plate number and informed him of what had happened. His remarks had made it easier for the police to track down Mario. I was not sure what he thought of this unusual outcome, but I was grateful to be able to tell him what I felt and to thank him. It was a little emotional for me because he had inadvertently helped me in a way in which he, or I, could never have imagined. For him, I think it must have been a strange and baffling encounter but he took my gratitude with grace and also took the opportunity to ask for a financial reward. Of course I was more than happy to give it to him.

I also planned to thank the woman who had helped me when I ran to the entrance of the estate where the twins were killed. I felt like I needed to express how her presence, clear-headedness, compassion and prayer had helped me. I always thought that she might have been called as a witness at the trial, but as it was not going to happen anymore I asked if I could get her number. I knew that I was not going to be able to talk so I sent her a message of thanks.

I told her how grateful I was that she stopped her car and

got out to help me. That she found the number to my son's school and dialled it so that I just had to talk to them. And how much I appreciated her praying over me, that it gave me a sense of protection, of safety, and above all else, of support, which at that moment I really needed. I remember that she replied, quite quickly, but am not sure what exactly it said.

It felt good to tell these strangers how they had helped me, what impact they had had, and how grateful I was.

In November 2019 I signed up to a yoga teacher training course taught by Jim Harrington. It was fascinating to meet so many interesting people. We learned not only about the specific yoga sequences, but about nutrition, chanting, meditation, breathing and Yoga Nidra which was completely new to me. There I met the beautiful soul, Karina Anderson. Karina had founded "The Smiling One Foundation", a fantastic project that helped prison inmates come to terms with their crimes, try to better themselves and become positive members of the community. She told me it took on average 4-5 years to complete the programme, but not one of those who had finished the course had reoffended.

I was astonished to discover that Mario had attended a Smiling One session. What did it mean? I got quite excited when I learned this from Karina as I thought maybe it signalled repentance and feelings of remorse. Was he trying to make amends? It was such a positive programme and I thought it was something I could tell César about that would help him in some way. But after making some enquiries I discovered that he had not attended by choice and that all inmates had to go to at least one session. However, it was unusual in that Mario was still awaiting trial and normally, only convicted inmates went through the programme.

One day I was talking to Karina and she mentioned that she helped victims by bringing them to talk to ex-inmates, who work for her, for support on their healing journey. This felt like something beneficial so I asked Karina if I could talk to some of her ex-inmates, to gain a better understanding of their reasons for doing what they did. I didn't know what to expect when we met at Karina's house. There, I was introduced to two ex-inmates and we sat round in a circle talking for about an hour.

I told them about my experience and they told me what they had done, what prison was like for them and how slowly they had realised how their actions affected their victims. These two were not murderers but robbers who had assaulted their victims. They talked about their regret and how the programme had helped them to work through their issues. These men were nothing like Mario. Their backgrounds were worlds apart, and their motivation for harming and traumatising was different. Afterwards I drove them to the bus station so that they could get back home and on reflection I saw that they were just ordinary people. If I had met them on the street I would never have guessed they had been to prison.

I was grateful to Karina for the opportunity to meet and talk with them. It helped me to come to terms with the fact that while there are evil people in this world, they are few. The vast majority of crimes were committed because of opportunity and need, or as a result of psychological problems or other hidden issues never properly addressed.

Sadly, justice systems are mostly punitive institutions, rarely equipped to rehabilitate offenders. There are very few places focussed on how to break the cycle of offending or how to make sufficient psychological change to fundamentally alter that person's outlook. I wholeheartedly believe courses like "The Smiling One" should be offered in all prisons.

To my mind, there exists the possibility of hope and redemption in us all, just as there exists in all of us the capacity for great good and great harm. And though you could say that Mario's death had made some things easier – it certainly made my family feel safer – it precluded the possibility that he might have taken the time within prison to look at himself and come to terms with his actions. If he had completed "The Smiling One" programme, for example, he may have been forced to look at what he had done, accept the consequences and feel some empathy for those of us he hurt most. He might have had an opportunity to feel remorse and find redemption. I would have wished that for him as a human being but above all I would have so dearly liked that to happen for César's sake. That would have helped him a great deal.

Finding Peace

*"I will no longer write these letters as I don't think
it's something I need anymore. I have achieved
what I set out to do, namely, finding a way through
the impenetrable grief."*

LETTER FORTY-SEVEN

I pick up the brush and let my hand take me where it wants
to go – one blue swirl forms the left hand side of the heart-
shape, sweeping downwards to form a point at the bottom.
Then I pick up the tip and move it back to the middle of the
plate. Now I move it in circles to make another swirl on the
other side, a perfect mirror image of the first.

Once it meets the point at the bottom I paint a sun in the
centre of the heart, then two long leaves, like arms, encir-
cling the heart. I am not much of a painter but I like the
design. Afterwards, I adorn the rim of the plate with flowers
and stems and let the ceramic paint dry. I glaze and fire the
plate, then I take it to the garage, place it carefully within the
folds of an old blanket.

And smash it to pieces with a hammer.

I learned about the art of Kintsugi a few years ago when I

came across an art piece that explained the process and philosophy behind it in a gallery. The words instantly resonated within me. Kintsugi means 'golden seams' and is the ancient Japanese art of mending broken pottery with gold paint, so as to emphasise rather than hide the breakage points.

The idea was that the item was not less valuable for having been broken, but more so, and its imperfections and flaws were to be celebrated as symbols of endurance and survival. That plate, or bowl or vase could never be the same as it was before. It was now a unique and beautiful item because it had shattered and survived. So I set about making my own piece of Kintsugi art and after I smashed the plate in the garage, I repaired it with gold paint.

Art is something that has helped me a great deal in the years since the twins were taken. I enjoy using my hands to create mini sculptures out of things I have found that might be broken or discarded. Any time we are near a beach I collect sea glass to take home to my studio. Old or shattered mugs, wine glasses, mobiles and all sorts of old pots and bits of jewellery have inspired me and given me ways to find new beauty in them. I like to see and appreciate objects that have been detached from their original purpose in a different way, to turn them into something new. Something even more beautiful and valuable.

At the moment I work a lot with resin. I don't always plan what to do. It just sort of happens between mixing and pouring. I like the process. It's slow but totally absorbing. After mixing the resin, you have to wait until it is a bit gooey because if you put the items in when the resin is just poured the dried flowers will just move around and you lose control of the work. Then you wait again until it's a bit harder to pour the next layer. I've done several pieces with pressed flowers and dead insects too, capturing something with life at the moment it was most beautiful and preserving it.

I have learned many things from losing Maximo and Octavia. I think that I was able to mould something with the broken pieces. The scars will always be present, but this different me is stronger, resilient, more patient and more aware.

Maybe I had to suffer this tragedy to realise it. I am learning daily, it will never stop, and I hope it never does. I think I would have reached this point without the trauma, but this has pushed me there faster. I was dropped in the deep end of the pool, and after a lot of struggling and near drownings, I am finally able to keep my head above water.

The shallow end is far away, but I am happy with the journey and where it is taking me.

Sometimes I wish I could revisit the past, to be more present with the twins and apply with them all that I have learnt. I want to hold them, feel and smell them, see them and hear them. I still get this intense yearning. I know there is no use, it only hurts me more, and the pain takes me back to the past, where nothing can be done. I often remember how I was unable to save them, and I feel deep despair. I can't help it. I still get guilty feelings of not having been enough for them. I could, and should, have done better.

But there is no point in reliving the past, I tell myself. There is nothing that can be done to change it and I accept that the guilt that accompanies these thoughts is inevitable and will probably live with me for a time to come. I'm not perfect, and that's fine. The point is to learn from my mistakes, any mistakes. Regrets appear to show us we have learned from our past. It would add to the tragedy if I had learned nothing from it.

The good thing is that these feelings come less and less, and they become less potent. Our emotions keep us anchored in the past. I used to feel myself being pulled down, and I could feel my body going into the same state I was in when I found them, or the days after when it felt like I was a walking zombie. It does get easier to recognise the feelings and emotions and how my body starts to slip. It gets easier to pull myself out sooner as I become more aware of my state. The flip side is that I am also more aware when I am in an elevated mood. And it helps me to remember these moments, to reinforce them, hands over heart, and to appreciate them.

In the beginning, I lived day to day, sometimes even hour to hour. I was glad at the end of the day, to have survived, more or less. Now I know, I am strong. Life continues, for which I am glad, and I no longer feel guilty for feeling that way either. It's fine to look forward to things. In the beginning, I looked forward to small things, like baking a cake, or going out for lunch, a weekend away. But every time things get bigger and further in the future.

I don't remember how long it took me to sing along to a song on the radio. I would just burst into tears, not only for the guilt of trying to feel something other than pain but also because it felt like a betrayal to their memory. Trying to enjoy something so simple, like singing, which was supposed to be done with feeling, was just too much. In the end, one just learns to live with it. I can sing a nursery rhyme now to Freya, my newborn daughter, and my heart doesn't ache with longing. I can do it and I'm pleased to be able to do it. I miss them every day and wonder what they would be like today but I am glad to feel joy and happiness again.

For a while I think I hid from my grief, letting it out only sporadically so that I could cope. It was too much to feel all at once. But I realised that if I did not feel all the so-called 'bad' or 'negative' feelings I would not be able to feel the ones on the other side of the coin: love, peace and joy. A person can't have one without the other. Anger, fear, guilt, despair, annoyance, loneliness, disgust and whatever else, are a part of life, just as love, peace, joy, gratitude, awe and inspiration are. All are natural responses and emotions. The hard part is not to allow the "negative" ones to pull us down and react to situations without thinking.

In the beginning, it was vital for me to know how they left this world. And maybe it is easy for me to say this now, as they went peacefully and quickly, but in the end, it does not matter. It is over for them. They are somewhere better. It was just me who was, and sometimes still is, reliving it and imagining the worst. I can never truly know what they felt, but that's okay. My imagination is better used somewhere else.

I think I have always had a large capacity to be able to accept 'shit' from other people. But at some point, inevitably, I would blow my top. With this new awareness, my capacity has increased. I'm not sure yet to which point, as my 'top' has not blown for a while, or it hasn't been as extreme as it was once before.

I have learnt much from this trauma. One is that things lose their importance, especially material things. I realised that many arguments were discussions about things that, in the end, were not important. It helped me to let go, to appreciate moments and people more. I was not able to control anything so I am better now at just running with it. Plans change at the last minute? Fine. No internet? Not the end of the world. Have to stay at home for months because of Covid? Okay. Change is inevitable, the more we fight it, the harder it is for us to accept.

I try to see any setbacks as teachers in disguise, to see what I can learn from the situation or crisis. There is meaning in tragedy. I learnt that no other person, no matter who it is, should ever have power over me. No person should make me suffer or affect my mood. I am in charge of my emotional wellbeing, of my internal state, no matter what mood another person is in, or what they say or do. I try not to let other people's low-frequency energies affect me. I am learning not to take it personally. Everyone is going through their own thing, and it has absolutely nothing to do with you. Even if someone does blame you, it usually has to do with their own insecurities.

Of course, we do take part of the blame, because of our own ignorance of their situation. But this gets complicated, and I don't quite understand it yet, as each one of us has our own perceptions, which guide decisions and reactions. How is one supposed to know what triggers a reaction of some type in someone else? I suppose the best one can do is to know in one's heart that we are guided by love, not by ego and judgement.

It is a misfortune that it took this considerable trauma to wake me up to these realities and become more aware and compassionate. We are human, and it is normal for us to feel emotions such as anger, fear and sadness. The critical point is not to allow them to rule us. Reacting to any situations with these emotions is what usually gets us into trouble. It is better to respond than to react. I try, but don't always succeed.

If and when I feel one of these emotions I try to remember to take a breath, or two, or three, before responding. Even if I miss the opportunity to respond to someone because it has taken me a while to calm down, analyse my reaction and understand the other person's point of view, I prefer that than to react in a way that creates more disharmony. In any situation, I try to think: *Is this helpful? Will my anger or my reaction to any given situation or person improve it?* Usually, the answer is no. It is hard – more often than not I feel I failed. But I realise that the more I try the better, or easier, it will become.

There is a realisation too that one will always carry this grief. You don't get over it. You learn to live with it. So then why is it such a taboo? Everyone has suffered some type of grief, why is there not more talk about it? I understand that it is hard, and, obviously, people prefer to talk about uplifting things, but it is a part of life: something that we will all face, more than once. Hopefully, not many have to suffer as I have. But there are many, infinitely many more, who have gone through much worse with less support. Some might feel that talking about it is like an invitation for bad things to happen. I might have thought the same way before, I don't think I gave it much thought. It is awful that this awareness only comes to me because of what I have been through.

Though I have always enjoyed rising early, over time I fell into a habit of getting up before 5am to write, meditate and do my exercises. I love this time of the day. It feels so peaceful. It is still my habit to get up early. It feels like these exquisite, precious hours before the dawn are the quietest and most delicate.

Many times I look up after my meditations to see the moon and stars bright against a clear black sky and later, the beautiful light orange and pink of sunrise changing second by second. I sense the earth waking up around me and hear the gentle sound of birdsong welcoming the daylight. It is magical. Before then, the peace and quiet just seem to have a different quality at that time. Being awake in that moment can set the tone for the rest of my day. I need to locate that peace and calm within before I face the world outside myself.

Keeping active has also helped heal me. To be out in nature, in the gym with weights, or swimming in the pool, or even better in the ocean, has been beneficial. And of course being creative has also helped along the way. I think most people would benefit, but what is most important is to find what each individual enjoys. We all need purpose. That is the key.

César, although very important, couldn't be the only thing

in my life. I couldn't put that on him. He deserved a mother who did not rely on him as a crutch. I needed to stand on my own. I need to use what I had been through, channel it for the good of others. That is what led me on the journey to write this book. I knew that if I could reach one other parent suffering the same pain as I experienced, made them feel less alone, then that would have been a worthwhile endeavour.

As Mother Teresa said: 'Parents who seek purpose and meaning from their tragedies can go on to do good, which then becomes part of their child's impact on the world.'

I still have a long way to go, but I am happy where I am and clearer on what I want, and more importantly, at peace with the process. I am enjoying the journey more than anything.

I am becoming more aware and patient. I have my off days, you can just ask my family, but even those off days are fine, as I learn from them. I trust myself more now. I know that everything will be fine, no matter what will come my way. I have survived the worst. I know the strength I have. And I know that everyone has that strength.

Everyone has different levels of awareness. We are doing the best we can with the level of awareness we have. We are not wrong. Our truth is our truth. It helps me to remember this when other people do things that they would not inten-tionally do. We might not be aware of what we do, or can't know how it could affect someone else, even with our best intentions. Awareness, I think, is vital. Not just of oneself, body, mind and soul, but awareness of the people we are surrounded by.

Why do I react negatively when things are not put back

in the right place? It comes from my need for control, but I cannot control the outside world, just what's inside. It is much easier (although still tough) to control our inner world than the outside. The power to feel better about any situation is within me. Like it is within everybody. It is something I still struggle with, but I am so much better than a year ago, or three years ago. Letting go is a big part, and a hard one, for a control freak like me. In this I don't always succeed. It's a long and windy road with mountains still to climb. But every day I try.

Awareness of the wider world is the next step. We are all connected. We are all one. We thrive when we are in communities, helping each other, of service, when and however we can. It is not easy, and sometimes that gets forgotten in everyday life. But to once in a while remember, and be aware, will make a difference. Sooner or later we become more mindful more often.

I remind myself to be patient with myself. Awareness and personal development take time. It is not something that happens overnight so I take baby steps and try not to expect too much of myself. Sometimes I feel like I have not progressed at all, other days, I suddenly realise how I reacted differently to a problematic situation, and how much I have changed. I notice how some things don't bother me as much. Or that I recover from setbacks much faster than before. It doesn't matter how small or insignificant they seem. Other days seem worse, but I know now how to get myself out of a slump. Every day is different but being patient and kind to myself is the first step. Happiness and sadness are not mutually exclusive.

As it is said, 'change is the only certainty in life'. One day you feel you need to know all the small details, later on, with time, you accept things with more ease and realise that many things are not as important as you first thought. I am learning to go with the flow, to find my path, and adjust the how, what and when as I move along it. In the end it's about choice. You choose how you react, what you feel and how you see things. You choose to listen to the angel on your left shoulder, rather than the devil on your right. You choose love over fear.

We have all suffered, we all want love. It is what connects us – family, friends and strangers. That is what we all share. That is what we all have in common. We all have the capacity for goodness and to see goodness in the world. If we were not, we would not be shocked and dismayed at the harm we do to each other.

I have one wish. For all sentient beings to feel love more often and more freely. Love has been around since the beginning of time.

Sages say that love never dies. It is eternal and will heal all wounds if we just let it. Not even death can erase it. Love overcomes everything.

Love is the bridge to our loved ones.

Letters To My Angels

Between June 2017 and April 2019 I wrote letters to my two lost babies – a way to channel the boundless love I had for them and to come to terms with their absence. None of the letters were dated but I kept them in order.

Here are those letters.

1

My dearest Octavia and Maximo,

You have been gone longer than three months (3 months and 19 days to be exact) and it hasn't gotten any easier for me. I don't expect it to. I miss you every day. Writing this brings me to tears. I am sorry if I have let you down. I put you in a situation of danger. I didn't know, and never imagined that your father would be capable of such a thing. I cling to the fact that you didn't suffer. At least, in that sense, I thank Mario. I don't know if I am still disconnected, but I still do not feel any anger towards him. I don't think about him much, nor the situation that he is in now. I just hope that when the trial comes, I don't say or do something that would decrease the number of years he gets in prison. Although I am not angry, I want and need him to pay for what he did to you.

It comforts me so much that you go and see Sam. This is the only direct connection I have now with you, and I treasure it deeply. I love you so much (I am crying again) and as Gary said, my love for you two has nowhere to go. Even when I have another child, it will be another love. Yours is yours, and I can't express it with hugs and kisses as you are not here. I can only express it with the love I feel and will always feel. Writing this brings me such sadness, I get this empty feeling inside, kind of like a big black hole. I also want to say that I am sorry for all the screaming I did, for being too strict and unyielding and not understanding you. I will probably be as strict with your brother or sister who will come along, but I will strive to be understanding and patient. I think I want to have another set of twins. I loved having you guys and want to experience that again. Maybe I'll do it better this time.

When I think about Mario's trial, I always go back to when I found you, and how I found you. It's difficult, and more often than not, I try to change my train of thought. But thinking about it is part of my healing.

As Gary said, it will be difficult, but not thinking about it and trying to suppress it, causes my anxiety to worsen. So now I try and write to you and talk to you. Hopefully, at some point, it will get easier.

I hope you two are at peace.

2

Hello, my angels.

I have gone back to dog training, and quite a few people have come up to me and given their condolences. There were tears, but I felt safe there. It helps me to know that you two are in the thoughts of other people as well. I don't want anyone to forget you. That is very important to me. As you only lived for three and a half years, which is such a short time, I don't want you to be forgotten by others. I will always remember, as will the rest of the family. But is that enough? I don't know. Maybe that's why I am so hellbent on getting my tattoo. People will be able to see it with ease when I'm not wearing long sleeves, and even though it might make people ask, I will get to a point where I will be able to say, 'yes, they died,' but I will also be able to talk about your life. At the moment I can't do this, especially without crying. Even thinking about it is bringing me tears now.

I am in the waiting room of Dr Penkin. I haven't seen her since you passed, and this will not be easy as she brought you into this world. She will take out the Mirena IUD, so hopefully, I can get pregnant soon. The first time of anything to do with you is always the hardest – your first birthday, the first Christmas, your first anniversary…

3

Hello, my two lovelies.

Today was a good day. I thought of you in a more positive

frame of mind, which, as you know, isn't the first time, but it's the first time I am writing about it. The pain is not so intense, it feels lighter somehow. César referred to you quite often today. He still looks at me to see if I'm going to start crying. He is too sweet. I was about to tell him that Iiro and I would start trying for another baby soon, but as it could take a while, I decided to wait until I am pregnant. He will be so happy. He misses you both so much. He liked your company and being able to play with you. He feels very lonely now, and although it will take at least another two years or so until he can play with his new brother or sister, he will enjoy every moment of being an older brother again. He will also hold them, feed them, and even change them, although I doubt that will be something that he would like to do. Iiro is excited about becoming a father. He will do wonderfully, I'm sure.

I love you, my Schatzies.

4

Hello again, my lovelies.

I have just watched a series in which one actor told the other that if he had a wish it would be that he could hug his daughter again, and that could never happen. I started crying immediately. That has never happened before. I can usually feel it coming. Now that I write it, that's not true; many times, the tears come without warning. I have just remembered that the first Christmas without you is coming up. That will be tough to take. I hadn't thought so far ahead. I just try to take one step at a time. I am looking at what's in front of me – today, tomorrow. Looking too far forward seems too hard.

5
—

Hello, my lovelies.

It has been a week since I last wrote to you. I am sorry I haven't written every day, I'm just not used to it, or maybe it's just an excuse, so I don't have to face my feelings every day. I don't think I am avoiding anything, but maybe I am not facing my reality. I suppose, as difficult as it is to admit, I just have to get on with it. There have been a couple of good days, but deep inside there is always something missing. I've been busy getting ready for our trip. César seems to be anxious about it for some reason, which worries me, but I will take him because I believe it will help. He says he does not want to miss anything fun or essential at school. Can that be it?

Gary said I should try to push César a little more to tell me about his feelings towards you and your father. I should explain the confusion I feel, and not put a label on it yet. César must feel just as confused and being unable to put his thoughts neatly into a box must be hard for him. I also have to ask him why he does not want to see me cry, and what he feels when he sees me doing that. I will explain to him that it makes me feel stronger and more at peace. I don't want him to bottle it up. He will have enough problems to go through when he gets older. I don't want him to have to face the grief later on. I'm more creative now, trying to make a birthday gift for Johan, and a costume for our holiday. I think it's helping me, it is what I enjoy doing. I have to learn to be happy with what I create and not be so critical.

I love you, my two, and I miss you every day.

6

Hello, my honeys.

The autopsy report said that you two were smothered. I am so sorry that he did this to you. I hope that Sam is right and that you were asleep when it happened. I don't want you to have suffered in any way. Anything that would have made your way over to the other side more stressful or scary would be difficult to bear. I am sure she is right and that he gave you some sleeping pills, or something similar, beforehand.

Maybe he did it so you wouldn't struggle, or because he didn't want you to suffer. I do believe that he loved you two. It's just that he hates me more, and you two were at the receiving end. I am so sorry about everything. I love you both so much and miss you always. It still feels strange to be at home with only César. You would be driving me mad now with your fighting and noise and asking for your iPads. I want that back.

I see your smiling faces in the pictures hanging on the wall, and every time it hits me that you are gone. It still feels like it is all a bad, long, nightmare.

7

My darlings,

Today was César's first day at Zip Zap Circus. I could not help and think that you would have loved it. I'm sure that if you had been here, you would have wanted to join in, or at least watch how César did. I don't think about what you would be like in the future if you had been given that chance. Maybe that is still something that will come. Perhaps it's just that because you were taken so early and so young, I can't imagine you grown up. This, in itself, is heart-breaking enough. What's worse, is not having seen you grow up, I can't picture you having children. If you had been more grown-up, and I could have pictured your future better. I would have had more memories. Mine are kind of blending now. I can now see Maximo dancing in the kitchen, and Octavia walking around pushing the pram and playing Mommy. I realised that the photos I took in February, March and April are missing. I keep thinking I should have taken more. I just went to watch some home movies of you. I hadn't done that in a while. How you enjoyed the beach the last time we were there. I miss you so much. I have too much time on my hands, although I complain that there are not enough hours in the day, although I don't even work.

8

Hello, my twins.

I saw another set of twins yesterday at the beach, saw how

they played together, and it broke my heart. I think that is why I want twins again. They have such a great connection to each other, even if they do fight. But in the end, you are never alone. That's what happens to any siblings, and also why I want another kid. César doesn't deserve to be on his own, even if the age difference will be significant, there is nothing like having a brother and/or sister.

Loss. That's a word that breaks my heart. I only truly understand the word now. The book I'm reading, *Healing After Loss*, keeps saying that after the storm comes the calm. We will be stronger and better in our new reality. I don't see it. I don't see a 'dampening' of my grief. It is getting quite difficult. Whenever I write you my heart breaks and I cry. I hope this will improve. How I would have loved to see you, Octavia, become a beautiful young girl. I keep remembering how you, Maximo, liked to dance and sing. I am sure that you would have done something that involves music. I think you would be the calmest of the three.

I love you and miss you both so.

9

Hello, my lovelies.

I found some images and videos on my iPad which I thought that I had lost. They are mostly of when we were all swimming in the pool, you two were with floaties and noodles swimming on your own— it's a bittersweet discovery.

Some days are hard, and others I can talk about you or about what happened and be quite alright with it. I think what hit me most was finding the videos and watching them. It's amazing how draining it is when you just cry for ten minutes. But it is also a release. Yesterday it took a while to feel that. I felt such deep sadness that it seemed to want to pull me down.

10

Good morning, my lovelies.

Iiro's friend Sam offered to guide us through a transcendental meditation today. I have been using the meditation app Headspace that Gary suggested, which was helpful, but this was great. I will research if we can do a TM course in Cape Town. I am getting better at being with myself and my thoughts, and have been for a while, but I think the meditation just seemed to show me that I needed to do more than what I was doing. I am very grateful that Sam guided us through this and opened my eyes to this new experience.

11

Hello again.

I haven't written to you in a couple of days as we are on holiday but there are things I want to tell you. On the evening of August 11, Iiro asked me to marry him. He proposed on the beach, it was beautiful. It was after I did some homework with César. He was not happy about that, and we struggled for nearly two hours. Afterwards, I was quite annoyed and felt like relaxing for a while. Iiro was about and always coming to check how we were doing. He suggested we take a walk to Turtle Beach. I didn't feel like it, but I thought he was trying to get my mind off the homework, and it would probably do me good, so we went. We had a couple of drinks at the beach. Then he suggested that we take a walk and look for a heart-shaped rock. I thought again that he was trying to get my mind off the stressful last two hours. After about 15 minutes he pointed something out, but I didn't react. When we retraced our steps, I looked to where he had pointed earlier and realised it was not a rock, and that it was split in two, I went over to pick it up and saw a ring. I turned to him in surprise. I only realised what was happening when I saw him on one knee. He asked, then he got up and we kissed. He asked me again if I would marry him. I said, yes.

On our way back, I asked him if marriage was vital to him, as I didn't believe in it anymore. I told him I wanted to spend the rest of my life with him, but I did not need a paper to say that we were married. We stopped and talked about it. He accepted my point of view, and although it was a blow to him, he took it graciously. We agreed to have a big wedding celebration and to pledge our love to each other in front of family and friends. But we wouldn't sign any papers. Being with Iiro is a choice I make every day, not because we've been bound together by a piece of paper, but because I want to. I realise it is not strictly what he wanted but it is the very most I can offer. I love Iiro with all my heart but I cannot ever contemplate being married again.

He had wanted to have the ring ready, but it wasn't, so he gave me a provisional one. It is lovely. His idea is to provide Misha with the gold he had mined in Lapland. He wants

Misha to make an infinity shape and break it in two so that we each get a half. It's a beautiful idea, and I love it. I can't wait to get the ring. César was the first person we saw, so we could tell him first. He was so excited!

12

Vicky and I, well, more Vicky than I, have been busy organising your birthday. The first birthday after your death. It will be hard. Before I left, we decided to collect and give to the four schools in Hout Bay's townships basic essentials like toiletries, food, blankets and other things they need. We selected two that needed help with repairs. At the school in Hangberg, we will paint tables and lockers, in Imizamo Yethu (one in the informal residential area in Hout Bay) we will put up railings for the curtains. We will spend the day doing that. The kids will enjoy painting. I am not sure what state I will be in. You would have turned four.

It's the first time I'm allowing myself to look forward and wonder what you would be like now. Toddlers change so quickly.

I had already noticed a change in both of you after you turned three. You were more understanding, able to accept things. Maybe it was just me, but it seemed to have gotten easier. Now I will never know what you would have turned out to be like. That still seems so strange to me.

Sometimes I still have to remind myself that you are both gone. It still feels like this should be happening to someone else, not to me. (I know that sounds awful!)

13

Hello, my darlings.

I have been suppressing my feelings all week, I was too busy running around, but I am sure that tomorrow will be difficult. I can't believe that almost five months have gone since you died. I miss you so much. I miss your cheekiness and sweetness, your screams and your hugs, how you enjoyed having your back scratched Maximo, and, Octavia, how independent you were. I wonder how you'd be talking now, and whether your personalities would be more evident. It's despairing that I will never get to see that, or to see what your hobbies, likes and dislikes would have been.

At one of the schools we went to, the kids had prepared birthday cards for you. It was tough not to cry when they came up and handed me the pink and blue cards. It took all the energy I had to smile and hold back the tears. I didn't want to break down in front of them. They were so sweet. But I was glad when it was over.

14

Hello, my beautiful twins.

I was anxious on your birthday. I cried quite a bit the day before, so I did not need to yesterday. We spent most of the day painting tables, cupboards and doors at Wavecrest school. I am glad we spent your day like that. César stayed for a sleepover at Vicky's house, which gave Iiro and me the chance to relax at home, to try to make a baby and watch some series.

When I was preparing dessert for our dinner, something remarkable happened. I was cutting strawberries, listening to Magic FM on the radio, when the song *I Will Always Love You* from The Bodyguard came on. At the same moment, the wind picked up and blew open the kitchen door. A wonderful warm breeze blew in and I just knew it was a message from the both of you. I thank you for that. It was comforting, and I appreciate any message you send me. I love you both so much. It is a great comfort to believe in the afterlife and know that you are well and at peace, that there is no fear or pain, just love.

15

Hello, my two lovelies.

I have been anxious because I received your autopsy report yesterday. There was nothing new in there, but there was a picture of you two lying on the bed, just as I had left you. I go over the day's events regularly, and that image always comes to my mind. But it's quite different when you see a photo. It's a natural and expected response, but not one I enjoy obviously. César went into his session with Yasmine, the child psychologist, quite positively. I do hope that he is getting better and that he will talk more openly soon.

Reading through some emails from Mario put me in a bad mood. César, who wasn't on his best behaviour, got the brunt of it, poor guy. I did say sorry before I left. I feel bad for leaving him. I was so excited before, but now I feel awful. Probably because I was not fair with him today. He certainly isn't to blame and I can't take it out on him.

I will soon have my tattoo done. I have high expectations and really looking forward to this as I will be getting my tattoo for you. Mr Cartoon will do it, the same guy who did my octopus tattoo. I know it will look incredible, but I'm scared I'm expecting too much.

16

I'm on the flight to LA. It's been a long day, but I am not as tired as I thought I would be. I suppose that walking to and from the airport gates has helped keep the sleepiness at bay. I am, thankfully, in a more or less hidden business class seat. I took out my book to read, but I felt the need to write. The last quote I read was this: 'They are alright. Return to the living, who need you.' I feel bad, guilty, for being able to do that. But I need to, mostly for César, but also for myself, and to show Mario that although he has broken me to pieces, I will find peace. It will come very slowly, but one day it will come. Another quote, there are so many in this book that call to me: 'But where my loved one is, a fragment of my spirit lives and waits.' It seems that lately, when I read, I cry. It wasn't always like that.

I will always love you, my beautiful babies.

17

Hello, my angels.
I have been in LA and the best part was getting my tattoo. I hope that you like it. It is a feather with flowers on one

half and your name and birthdates above it. It was Iiro's best friend Roma's birthday so we went to the Italian restaurant, Madeo, to celebrate.

At dinner I sat next to our friend Jeremy. When he said how sorry he was, I teared up, just like him. It always seems to happen when people offer me their condolences. Now I will have to get used to it as people will see my tattoo and your names will be out there.

18

Hello, my angels.

I went to Murcia, in Spain, for my school friend Laura's wedding. It was nice to see all my closest friends together again. It seemed surreal to not be talking about you.

I was obviously asked how I was, but there seemed to be an unspoken understanding that there would be no talk about you, or what happened. It was strange, and also slightly freeing.

My thoughts were never far from you, but it seemed that I did need to let them out.

At some point as I was talking to a friend of Laura's, who also had twins, and I could not stop myself. Poor guy, I must have left him standing there reeling. I had a realisation that hit me while I was at the hotel. When I think of you two, I have a moment of utter despair before the sadness and tears come.

When the tears don't come, there is sometimes more despair, but every so often it's a little lighter.

19

I am on my last flight home. I was finally able to cry on the plane. I had feelings of guilt coming up, for flying so much in what was the last year and a half of your lives, for shouting when you were crying, for not connecting more with you, Octavia, and for not being a better mother, because you deserved the best and I didn't give it. I am so sorry, my angels. I still wish you were here and that I could see you grow up, so I could make up for my bad parenting. I want to show you that I can do better. You don't know how sorry I am that I left you in an unsafe place. I didn't know or even suspected that your father was capable of such a thing.

I miss you so.

20

Hello, my angels.

I'm not writing as often, and for that I am sorry. I don't seem to get any time to myself when I can write in peace. As I usually start crying, I like to be alone. I'm not ashamed of crying, but I don't want other people to feel sorry for me. I don't want to have to stop and explain. And although I want everyone to know about you so that you won't be forgotten, I also don't want to drop this kind of bomb on someone I don't know. I always find it challenging to decide how to respond to people who don't know me when they ask me how many children I have. Inevitably more questions will come and at some point I will have to say that you two are dead. Having your twins killed by one's ex-husband is a giant bomb to drop on someone. I don't want them to feel bad when I start to cry. Sometimes I don't cry. Some people have said sorry for asking, as if bringing it up was reminding me of you two. They don't know, and I don't hold it against people.

I am sure that in the past I have not responded appropriately to questions. In the end, what I have realised is that there is no right way to react. Not everyone wants the same thing. If they're going to talk about it and ask questions, I am usually alright with it. I have never told anyone that I did not want to talk about it, because it hasn't happened, but I know that people would understand if I did. It's not their fault. Usually, the tears come when I talk about you, think about you and remember you, but then again, not always. There is nothing usual about this. When I do cry there are tears now, not uncontrollable sobs.

At my session with Gary we talked more about Mario. As I did not see Mario at the bail hearing, I wanted to talk about the uncertainty of my feelings towards him. As I have said, I don't feel the anger. I think I should feel something. But strangely I feel nothing for him. Talking to Gary helped me realise that since the separation I learned that the less I am hurt by what Mario said or did, the better it is for me, and the less power I give Mario. This probably angered him more, but I believe that he would have done what he did sooner or later. And as awful as it sounds, I think Sam is right, it was better sooner than later. If you had been older, it would have been worse for you. Now I will probably have to wait more than a year to see Mario. It might be more difficult by then, but, as Gary said, I can face him "virtually". I don't have to have him in front of me to face whatever demons are hiding inside me, if any. I need to face the little girl inside me and see what she faced and how she is hurting, to help her heal. Hopefully, I can do this and be strong enough to face whatever is coming.

I did what Gary suggested. I didn't really know what to expect. The whole idea seemed strange. But when I imagined the me now giving a younger me a hug, with love and under-standing, and no judgement, I had a sense of safeness and comfort come over me. Tears streamed down my face, but it felt more like a release of having been seen and acknowl-edged.

I found a place close to home where I can do a meditation course. Iiro decided to do it with me. It's a small group of eight people and learning to meditate in this way is lovely. Being in the group makes it easier, it helps me somehow. The first time I meditated, I went in quite deeply, since then I haven't as much. It might be because, after the three days of group meditation, we now do it at home. It seems to be easier for Iiro to go deep. Maybe I have more issues to get through. Or maybe it's difficult to still my mind. It doesn't matter really. Everyone has their own pace and their cobwebs to take out.

21

Hello, my angels.
Today marks the six-month anniversary of your death. I feel

such a deep sense of despair. It still hits me like a sledgehammer. It always seems unreal that this has happened. There are no words that can describe the loss I feel. I was a bit down yesterday, as I think subconsciously I knew today was coming. I don't mark the days and don't expect the anniversaries with fear, but they hit me suddenly with the realisation that I have survived six months without you in my life. I've had great days, and many good ones, which makes it all the more challenging.

In the afternoon I picked up César and went straight to the bike park. I remember the last time I was here with you two and thought how you would like it now. There are so many kids you would have made friends with. While César was riding, I read my book. As always, many quotes resonate with me, but this one made me smile: 'Having no alternative… I will trust life with what I cannot know.' Sadder are these: 'The love emanating from my memories is eternal." And: "Love is the heartbeat of all life.'

Will I recognise you when I see you again? Tears stream down my face and I wipe them away quickly so that César doesn't see, it would just make him sad.

22

Hello, my angels.

I just finished another session with Gary. We were talking about the anger that I am not feeling towards your father. Right at the end, I remembered that sometimes I do imagine situations where I would get angry. But Mario is never there.

It's always towards someone else, not someone I know, but someone who has done something terrible. Maybe it's because this person is threatening to hurt César or someone else close to me. I imagine becoming a lioness. But I soon realise that that is not me. I might say something in anger, but that would upset me and I'd quickly retreat into myself, just as I did when I discovered you.

I have started a 30-day yoga challenge. I've done only three days, but I feel good. We will see if that continues, it seems a bit too much to do yoga every day. And it might also bring out stuff. I also might be anxious as I want to be pregnant, and I don't know yet if I am. This waiting game is probably not helping matters, only three more days until I hear. I am sure it will be difficult, but it is the right choice and will be good for everyone. I love you two so much, and there isn't a day that goes by that I don't think of you two. You are always in my mind, and especially in my heart. Always in my heart.

23

Hello, my angels.

Yesterday was a hard day for me. My anxiety returned during the yoga session, but I went to see Emma to do TRE exercises (Trauma Releasing Exercises), which helped. Afterwards I went to meet Jo, the lady who is doing your mosaic chairs. She did the mosaic sign at the entrance to My Montessori. They are very happy to place some chairs in the school garden in memory of you. Jo showed me the design for the two chairs, one for each of you. Your bunnies are at the centre, sitting in a field of flowers, with butterflies and a rainbow at the back. Your names are discreetly placed on the sides of the chairs. I love them.

We met at your old school. I didn't think it through and didn't realise what effect it would have on me. As soon as I drove through the gates I realised I hadn't been back since the last time I picked you up from school. It was the first time I had been back since you had died. It was tough. When I saw the kids playing in the garden, it broke my heart. I just remembered the many times I went to fetch you, and how much you loved being there. I broke down twice and decided to leave as it was just too much. Later I contacted Jo and asked her to do another chair for home, with both bunnies together. The design looked so lovely I wanted one for me as well.

Tomorrow I will take a pregnancy test. I am looking forward to it. I think I am pregnant, but maybe it's just wishful thinking. I will also see Sam. Her sessions usually come when I need to hear something even though I don't know what it is I need. I'm reading a new book called *Option B*. I like it, but it's very different to *Healing After Loss*, which was also excellent. The last phrase in the introduction is: 'Life is never perfect. We all live some form of Option B. This book is to help us all kick the shit out of it.' I know that I am not totally to blame for what happened to you, no one ever thought he would be capable of it, but I do share the blame. 'Not everything that happens to us happens because of us'

24

Hello, my angels.

My pregnancy test showed positive! I am going to have a baby. I worry if the baby will be healthy, that maybe I'm moving too quickly. Will the foetus suffer from my anxiety? And then there is the trial to contend with.

Iiro has left for three weeks. I will be on my own for a while. It will be nice. I miss you, my babies. I'm watching documentaries on Pollsmoor, the prison where Mario is being held. It makes me think of you. It makes me think of the kids whose fathers are in there, the children on the streets, and those who end up there. I am glad you had a better start in life, and I am so sorry it ended like it did. It is still hard for me to accept that you are gone. It also makes me realise what Mario must be going through. And being the person he is, he must be taking it very badly. I wonder how Mario thought his plan was going to work out. Did he think he would get away with it? Did he want to get away with it?

When I first told Iiro, over pizzas at the Red Herring in Noordhoek, that I was more than likely pregnant, he stayed relatively calm. Yesterday, when I drove him to the airport and told him I was sure I was pregnant, he got very excited. I regret I did not tell him in a better way. I know that this will be my last child, but for him it will be the first. I should have made it more special. I think it's the first time I've been pregnant and not told everyone about it. It's strange to keep it a secret, but I suppose that as soon as I am out of Dr Penkin's consultation room, I will be calling many people.

25

Hello, my angels.

At yoga my tears just started to flow. I held back a bit because I felt that I would start sobbing if I let go. I went to see Emma where I finally did some TRE and trembled. I think I might be a bit anxious. I told Gary I was not looking forward to Christmas because you two would not be here. You spent the last two Christmases with your father. It makes me sad that I was never able to enjoy them with you.

César has taken over your room, so his old room will be the baby's room. Yes, I am pregnant, the blood test has confirmed it. I am sure it will be a boy as I am sleeping well and have no nausea. Do I have twins? I don't know yet. I am still undecided if it would be a good thing. Yes, it was difficult, but enjoyed having you two and I loved being your mother. But maybe having twins again would be too much.

26

Good morning, my angels.

As I was driving back from dropping off César at school, towards my yoga lesson, I cried again, like so many other times. I miss you so much. I haven't looked at your pictures for a while, and when I do, it hits me that I haven't seen those beautiful faces in such a long time that I am starting to forget. There were a few videos of Maximo dancing in the kitchen, wiggling his bum, he was so cute, I remember it so well. Will I forget with time?

27

Hello, my angels.

I realised yesterday why my anxiety usually starts on a Tuesday. It's the combination of yoga and seeing Gary. Later, Sadi saw me crying. She hasn't seen me crying for a while. I think it took her by surprise. She misses you both. Today the weather reflects my mood. It's rainy and a bit misty. I went to buy some yellow and purple daisies for you.

28

Hello, my angels.

I saw Dr Penkin for a scan. I knew I was pregnant, but it was nice to see that little bundle of cells. I am happy. I am quite sure it will be a boy. Sometimes there is a hint of morning sickness, which is why I think it might be twins. But I might be wrong again. Maybe it's a girl. As long as the baby is healthy, I don't mind. What I feel strongly about is that both kids out-live me. I don't think I will survive another funeral of a child of mine. It still takes me by surprise. It sometimes even seems like having had you was a dream. I miss you both so much. I wonder what you would be like now. Already past four, I can imagine what naughty things you would be getting up to. Probably fighting with César but playing together as well. It would be a loud house again. I sometimes even miss that. I am so sorry that this happened to you and that you could not grow up and enjoy the world as you had every right to. I am so sorry it was cut so short. I love you two so much.

I went today to a stained-glass maker who will make a plaque for your memorial room at the Zip Zap Circus studio. I think it will look great and I'm glad I thought of it. They will make it much better than I could have.

29

Hello, my angels.

Today we fly to London to see the family. I will tell everyone that we are pregnant. They will be happy, but you two will be missed, as always. I will be staying a bit longer for meetings, some classic car racing and seeing friends. Hopefully, I can also go shopping for pregnancy clothes. I look forward to seeing Kaivi, who recently lost his sister. I will give him a copy of the book *Healing After Loss*. I hope it helps him and his family. I'm reading a new book now, *Grief Works*, and here is the first quote that echoes within: 'We must find a way of living with a reality that we don't want to be true.'

Another one: 'The paradox of grief is that finding a way to live with the pain is what enables us to heal.' César has been my primary motivation for a long time. I can still feel the utter despair I felt when I found you. And that more than anything brings tears to my eyes.

30

Hello, my angels.

I am at Bodhi Khaya, in Stanford in the Western Cape Overberg, on a yoga retreat. It's beautiful here. I am on my own, so I'm not sure how that will be for me. I seem to prefer to be around friends and family, but it will be okay. After lunch, I was sunbathing by the lily pond, and maybe it was my imagination, but I think I felt your presence. I always imagine, especially when I am in beautiful places, how much you would like it. I missed so much in your last year and I regret not being there. I know you were okay and loved being with Sadi, but this was precious time that I will never be able to make up. I know you don't hold it against me, but sometimes I feel so guilty. I hope that I am better now with César and will be more present with my fourth baby. I hope I can learn from my mistakes. I hope that you felt loved by me. I do feel loved by you, now and always.

Last night at dinner, I told two women I don't know about what happened. I was nervous, hot and shaky. I always feel conflicted. It's a strange battle that seems to go on inside me. I need people to know about you two, but I don't want the attention on me. I need it to be on you. I don't want you to be forgotten. At the moment I don't think it's enough that I, my family and friends, hold you in our hearts. I want the world to do so as well. No child should ever be forgotten.

I miss you so much.

31

Hello, my darlings.

It upsets me sometimes that I don't cry so much anymore. Am I just getting used to the pain and loss, or have I cried so much that I no longer can? But then the tears do come. Not as hard and as quickly as before, but they come. Oma told me the other day that she always says that she has ten grandchildren, including you. When I am asked, I always say I have just one child, César. Not that I don't want to acknowledge you, I do, but I still worry about the questions that may follow, and the explanations I will have to give. This, again, is a contradiction, as I want everyone to know about you so that you are not forgotten. But I think I will say from now on that I have three, soon four. And if further questions are asked, I can say that two of my four are in heaven.

As you can see, I am conflicted about this. I will just have to see how it goes. The tears are flowing freely now, they come mostly when I write to you, and I'm not doing that enough. This morning I did Budokon yoga for the first time. Before the class, the teacher, who taught me SUP yoga, asked about the two of you. I explained and then quickly changed the subject. I probably do that a lot, either because I believe I help the other person feel less uncomfortable, or so I don't feel uncomfortable. Or maybe it's just me and my perception. How they see it might be quite different. It's all very confusing.

32

Hello, my angels.

Yesterday I had a significant day that was bittersweet and sad. Firstly, when I collected César from school, he had a small oval-shaped bowl that I told him was beautiful and that I loved. It reminded me of the last day I saw you, which was when he made it. We had gone together to pick César up from his birthday party and I then drove you to your father's rented apartment. Although it was the last day I saw you alive, you still had three weeks of life. If only I had known. I started crying when I explained it to César. He looked so sadly at me. Later that day I started to bleed and lost the baby I was carrying. I was upset, but after the loss of you two, this did not seem as bad. And as I don't have trouble getting pregnant, I know I will have another child soon. I have been through so much, and much more is still to come. That it is probably why I lost the baby.

I miss you guys. I love you always.

33

Hello, my angels.

Today it's been eight months. It's incredible how quickly time goes, even when you feel it dragging. Monday was a super moon, and I've been feeling slightly more apprehensive and depressed since then. Yesterday we went to your school to inaugurate the chairs. The kids from your school love them. They are beautiful, so colourful and comfortable. César loved them too. I look forward to having our one in the garden soon.

34

Hello, my angels.

I talked with Sadi today. She misses you so. She is struggling quite a bit. Moses as well, but as he does not communicate as much, it's difficult to know with him. She repeated some of the things she had told me before, which had not registered because I couldn't handle it at the time. She said how Mario treated you differently, not with the same love and affection that he showed César.

Before, I believed that everything was fine, that he was a good father because you missed him, and always seemed happy when you talked to him over Skype. But knowing that your final weeks were not great and that your father did not show you the love he should have breaks my heart.

Sadi also reminded me how you would call her "my Sadi" and how she called you "my princess" and "my prince". You loved her.

35

Hello, my angels.

We arrived in St. Moritz for Christmas holidays yesterday. I haven't been here for two years, and I am glad to be back. It brings memories of when you guys were here.

I keep thinking how much you would enjoy it now. You would be old enough to learn to ski, ride on the sleigh and enjoy the winter snow. There is not a moment I don't miss you and think of you. I realise that if you were alive, you would be with your father, but I would have brought you here for a week at least. I miss having you around. I miss having twins. César was great today with Charlie, his little cousin, and played with him often. He will make a great big brother again. He misses you. We all do.

36

Hello, my angels.

It seems I haven't written to you in a while, but it's only been a few days. Nothing much has changed. Christmas is drawing near, and I try to avoid thinking that you two won't be here. It's not the first time that I won't be with you for Christmas. Unfortunately, I missed the last two, but as César will be with me, it will be a strong reminder that you are no longer with me. It's the first Christmas you are no longer of this earth. That still is a strange thought for me, although slowly I seem to be getting used to the idea. In two days, it will be bad for me. I miss you so much. I hope you are doing well, my loves.

37

Merry Christmas, my angels.

I'm so sorry you are not here with us. Yesterday was a difficult day for me. Being Christmas, made it worse. Christmas is remarkable when you have kids. It makes it all so much more magical to see the expressions of wonder and excitement. We opened presents with everyone around the tree. I was fine, but suddenly I realised that I needed to escape and be alone. I made it to my room before I started to cry. It was not for long, and after a while, Iiro came to check on me. I feel that although the crying is becoming further apart, it seems deeper somehow. I remembered the last time we walked up to El Paradiso for lunch. You, Octavia, had a screaming fit, and it took me a while to calm you down. In the end, we had a nice lunch there.

It is difficult to understand how a father can do that to his children. It's also hard to work out why his hate for me was so great, I wish he would have hurt me in another way, but he knew this would be the most effective. I miss you always.

38

Hello, my loveys.

It's a new year (2018) and I haven't written to you for a while. We flew back home and had a quiet night in. We just made it to midnight to kiss each other for the New Year and then fell asleep. The days are relaxed at the moment. Sadi is not here, and although most things are open, the big companies are still on holiday. César was quite sick yesterday but seemed to have gotten over the worst. I think I am now coming down with something. It would be better if it happens now, rather than later, when César goes back to school. I find it so strange to think that in three days it will be nine months since you died, three quarters of the year. It seems to have flown by. I still can't believe you are gone. It doesn't take me by surprise anymore, not really. I just can't believe that I belong to the group of people who had to bury a child of theirs. Even worse, two at the same time, because of a heinous act.

39

I love you, my babies, so much.

Today César meets his new teacher, and I can't help thinking that if you hadn't died, you both would be starting at Hout Bay International. It's not an easy day. All of these firsts are very difficult. The first Easter without you, the first summer holiday, birthdays, Christmas, and first time starting big school. The worst will be the first anniversary of your death. I feel the grief is not as shocking anymore. I'm getting used to it, I suppose. I am learning to live with it. There is a before you died and an after.

I am doing quite a few craft things, which helps me handle life better. I feel more at peace after working on something. I don't know if it will ever be anything more than making presents for my family, but that's not the point. The basic things help me the most – doing what I enjoy, exercising, being in nature and reading. It was good that Iiro and my family forced me to do things. I don't know if they realised that they were forcing me, but it took all I had to get up and do them. It helped not to lie in bed all day, which is what I desperately wanted to do. Everyone is different, I suppose, and has their own way of moving forward, but the point is to move forward. In the beginning the steps were so small and seemingly insignificant that I did not realise what I was doing.

40

Hello, my angels.
Your first anniversary is coming up sooner than I realised. I will ask everyone to bring something that reminds them

of you, or something small that they want to give or dedicate to you. We will put it together on a board in a picture frame I have prepared before having lunch, enjoying Vicky's daughter Cyann's chocolate cake and two different types of bubbles, the ones that you like to play with, and the other for the adults to drink. It will be a difficult day for everyone, but hopefully not too sad.

One of the mothers from your school organised your classmates to draw pictures for you. They gave me a folder full of those drawings. I could see how those kids were already drawing more lifelike stick figures. They had reached a point that you two never got to, and something as simple as that is too much for me. But I treasure it and am grateful for it. I try to imagine what you two would be drawing.

41

Hello, my angels.

I've been looking at your pictures a lot today, and I seem to be more sensitive than usual. I suppose it's also because I haven't cried for a while, and although I think of you always and look at your pictures daily, the tears do not always come, I don't know why. A picture came up on Facebook of you two sitting outside the kitchen eating ice cream with César. I remember that so well. It seems so long ago.

I've had an extended break from writing to you. It helped me a lot in the beginning, now I don't cry when I write. I suppose I am more at peace, but it doesn't feel like it. Or maybe I don't want to be. I miss you. Maybe grief is evolving. I might not cry as much but the feelings remain. The pain of losing you is with me, as is the despair and the love. I am sitting by the pond. Iiro is in LA and César is happily on his iPad. I will soon go in and start working on a mosaic mirror, but I wanted to write to you more than just a few sentences. I finally have time and peace, but more importantly, I remembered to write in the diary. I'm always thinking of you, but somehow writing it down in the diary escapes me. And when I do, it's usually never a good time.

This time last year you were already with your father. In two weeks it will be the first anniversary of your death. It is incredible, it feels like it was only yesterday. I'm thinking more and more about what you would be like now. You would both be talking non-stop I'm sure. You would be enjoying school, fighting and playing with César. I would be going up the wall. Iiro would be with us. It would have been perfect. What beautiful little children you would be now.

César had a small breakdown after I put him to bed. While Iiro and I were meditating, I could hear him walking about. He came down to see us, but when he realised we were meditating, he left us alone. I finished my meditation and went to talk to him. He was sitting in front of your pictures and crying. That broke my heart. He misses you so much. We sat there for a while and then I put him to bed. I lay down with him for a time. Suddenly he asked if it was hard for me and in what way. I told him that I miss you every day, that I wonder what you would be like now, how grown-up you would be, and how much you guys would be talking, laughing and fighting. He said he wondered what you guys would feel like. I didn't get it, I thought he meant what you would feel yourself, but he was referring to what he would feel when he touched you. I showed him that your skin would be as soft as the inside of his arm. We stayed together for a little while longer. He slept with the light on and your picture in front of him. He slept with the picture for a couple of nights. I hadn't seen him cry for a while, and I was happy that he was releasing a bit. He should do it more often. It's difficult because he doesn't understand and bottles it up. But if I push too hard, it shuts him down further. He has to do it on his own time. He has been much happier. He is getting better. But a big hole remains in all of us. It's something that will never go away.

We finally know that the trial will start a week before you would have turned five. I'm glad we have a date at last, but it's still a long way away. I love you, my angels.

42

Hello, my angels.

Yesterday César had movie night at school, and when I went to fetch him, he was having a pillow fight with some of his classmates. They were having lots of fun, but I was tired and cold. It was late as well, but he asked me if he could stay a bit longer, so I gave him a few more minutes. When it seemed that the kids were leaving, I told César to pack up and come home. Just as we were leaving, the kids started playing again, but I made César leave. He was not happy about it and sulked to the car. I let him be, but after a few minutes of driving, I realised that he was crying. I explained that having a pillow fight was great fun but that it was late and we had to go. All the other parents were getting their kids ready as well, so they were not going to be playing for long. He then said it wasn't about that. I realised that he was crying about you. It always seems that when he is a bit upset about something, he starts crying about you. It's kind of his door opener. But this time he was crying very hard and sobbing. I stopped the car on the side of the road to comfort him.

He said that he was a bad brother and that it was his fault that you had died. He said that he was not for this world. This worries me as he said something similar a while back. Once he said he wanted to Google how one can kill oneself, and right after you two died he said he wished that it was him instead of you. I don't think he will ever do anything like that because he is too young, but I will bring it up a few times to make sure that he is not always thinking about it. Back in the car, I comforted him and said that he was an seven-year-old boy, it was not his job to keep the babies safe. I told him it was my responsibility, and it should have been his father's. And I also told him that he was a great brother to you.

Of course, you guys fought, that is normal, you also played together, he took care of you when he was able to, he read to you, and he loved you. And the important thing is that you guys knew that. I suppose he has a bit of survivor's guilt. I will wait a few days, or a week, and then get him another appointment with Yasmine. We have not been to see her since the last term. He seems happier than the previous few months, I thought it was good for him to have a little break. I can't make the appointment too soon because I don't want him to think it is a punishment for opening up to me. He was quite happy this morning, for which I am grateful. He does not seem to linger in a depressed mood, which I take as a good sign, but he might be good at hiding it.

You are both missed so much by everyone. I can't wait to be able to tell César he will be a big brother again. I think he will be a wonderful brother, just like he was with you. I am also glad that he is old enough to remember you. Probably not so well, as time goes on, but he will have some memory. If it happened when he was younger, he would not remember as well, and I think that would hurt him more in the long run.

43

Hello, my angels.

I've been doing a different type of healing these last ten days or so. I've been reading Beyond Willpower, and the other day while doing the exercises it suggests, I had a wonderful experience. I placed my hands in three different positions. First over my heart, then over my brow and lastly on the crown of my head. While doing that I repeated, "Great Light, please heal all negative issues, beliefs, memories and energies from my conscious and unconscious mind. Please heal all my fears from my conscious and unconscious mind and replace it with love, peace and joy." I repeated that three times over each position.

Two nights ago, when I did it, I got amazing visual effects.

The first time over my heart, I got colours, red for love, yellow for peace and blue for joy. When I did it over my brow I had images of you two and our dogs that had also died. For Peace, I saw images of the sun and being in a meadow. My face also became quite hot. For Joy, I saw images of water. When I placed my hands over my crown, the images got more focused, but at the same time, harder to discern. And there were so many images I am not sure what I saw. I did it yesterday again, but it was not so intense. It was not the aha moment the book describes, but it's something. I am not doing exactly as the book recommends, and I have not finished reading it yet. I do feel more relaxed, and I think I don't get as annoyed over trivial things as I did before. But it has only been a few days. I am not sure if the effects will last, and whether my past fears will dissipate.

I seem to have a bit of anxiety again. Maybe it's because I am working through my fears subconsciously, or because yesterday Jay from Dream Weavers came by to design a jungle gym in your memory at Bel Ombre park in Constantia. It's still only an idea that I have, but it's moving slowly forward. Whenever something directly related to you is about to happen, I seem to get anxious. I started the process in about October last year. I finally got a reply about a week ago from the City Council allowing me to do it! Better late than never. It won't be big – just a slide, swing, climbing pole and a bridge – but something for the local children to play on. During meditation I keep thinking I need to do something to be of service in some way. I do know that I need to give back in some way. I just need to figure out how. And what.

I think of you so often, and the last few days I've also been crying more. It's always a bit difficult to discern why it's happening, whether it's all connected or if it's anxiety and sensitivity because of something else. I am more sensitive at the moment. It seems that my emotions are closer to the surface and easily disturbed. I don't know why. There is nothing new or different at the moment. The trial date is getting closer, so it could be that, but I hope that does not mean that it will get worse. It might, and that's ok. I know I will get over it. The pain of losing you does not diminish. My despair is always the same. I know that my life has to go on for César's sake and mine, but the guilt is sometimes too much at the moment. Was I so awful to Mario that I was able to drive him to do something so despicable? I do wish that I had seen you alive for a last time. It eats at me that I could not hold you, see you, and kiss you before you were taken from me. Maybe if I had, I would have realised something, or at the very least held you one last time. I can't wait for the trial to be over.

I love you so much, my angels.

44

Hello, my angels.

I am writing to you from the parking lot at Constantia Village. We were robbed the other night. I was home alone, César was having a sleepover, and Iiro went to Clifton for a boys' night with his friends. I've been suffering from anxiety since Friday and stayed up late to see if I would calm down enough to go to bed. That only happened at around

2am. I was so tired by that time that it didn't matter if I was anxious or not. I went to bed and kept all the dogs inside as it was raining. At some point, I heard Lilly barking, and I shouted at her to stay quiet. In the morning, I had breakfast and cleaned up.

Then I headed to the office as I wanted to get to work on my projects. I realised something was strange, and noticed my computer was gone. I looked around and saw other things missing. When I saw that the TV was gone, I realised that we had been robbed.

I called Iiro to let him know, and he hurried back. But I felt fine. The guys who did it did not break a thing. And even though it was raining, there was not a drop of mud or water anywhere. It was probably someone from the construction site next door, but I am sure that no one will be found and that our stuff is gone. No matter, we are insured, and I understand that this is food for those thieves for the next few months. I'm not sure if I would have reacted differently before. It seems unimportant, though. I am thankful that Iiro was not home. He would have reacted to the dogs' barking and would have investigated. Who knows how the robbers would have reacted? And if César would have been there as well and woken up? I don't want to imagine. He would have become more traumatised than he already is. He is already scared of robbers coming into the house.

My anxiety isn't getting any better. I had to force my breathing, but it made the anxiety worse. I went to see a GP who gave me some medication to make it much more manageable.

45

My angels,

I suspect that I am pregnant again. I went to have the blood test done before booking an appointment with Dr Penkin. She then called to give me the good news. This time Iiro and I decided to keep it a secret. More than anything, César was so disappointed when I lost the first one that we didn't want to get his hopes up. The tricky thing will be to keep this quiet. I have always told everyone as soon as I knew I was pregnant. When we go out with friends or see Vicky and Johan, I will have to have a drink in my hand and pretend to enjoy it so that no one suspects. Iiro said that would not be a problem, he would drink mine and keep handing me his empty glass. I think he might rethink that plan after the first few lunches and dinners.

46

My dear ones,

This year for Christmas we are in Finland to spend time with Iiro's family. I know it is nice to do something different and to see more of where he grew up. But I think every significant holiday will be hard from now on, not being able to share it with you. It is difficult being away from my family. I didn't realise it would be like this. Iiro's family are great, but I miss you. I wonder how you would look, and what you would be like.

I have been writing less and less as I have not felt the need.

Although I was never very eloquent, it was beneficial in the beginning to write down what I felt. I know I could have spoken to Iiro, my parents or my sisters, but it always felt easier to write it down.

47

Dear angels,

Our daughter Freya was born a week ago. I had to have a C-section. She seemed quite happy to stay but the placenta was calcifying, and as I had a C-section with you guys, I could not be induced. It is incredible how differently the body re-acts to each baby. Maybe it's because she is my fourth, but there is no pain when I breastfeed her. I hope this continues.

It is such a difference to have a child with someone who is present and helpful. Iiro can't do much at the moment as Freya is breastfeeding and sleeping, but he is a burp master and goes shopping and helps take care of us all.

It is also amazing how easy it is. César was my first, so that was unnerving as I never knew if I was doing it correctly or not. Mario was never of any help. You were more straight-forward because I had the experience and confidence, but there were difficulties having two. I am always thankful that I had César before you. I don't know how first-time parents of twins cope. With Freya, I know more and am much more comfortable. It could also be that she is an easy baby.

It surprised me that it did not hurt as much as I expected. I knew that having another baby would remind me of you and what you were like at the same age, but I thought the memories would be more painful. Instead, although sad at times, I was so happy to remember things that I had forgotten: the first few weeks of your lives, how I fed you both at the same time, sleeping forehead to forehead in a shared crib, the half-winks and little smiles that Maximo used to make. Later, when he was about three, he learned to wink properly.

The playground is now complete. I had an idea for a plaque for it: 'In memory of all our little angels who were taken too early.' But when I saw an article in our local paper about the playground being built in your memory, it seemed that that was enough. I didn't need a plaque. I realise it is no longer so important to me that all these other people should know and remember you. It is enough that the few we are, will remember. It doesn't have to be the whole world.

Although my letters to you both have been patchy and short, they have helped me to heal, to come to terms with what happened, and to learn to live with the pain. I was not eloquent in my writing, which is fine, but now when I read through the letters again, it seems that I was not able to really express my feelings and emotions. Whichever way I put it, the words failed to convey all I felt, and still feel. It is indescribable.

I will no longer write these letters as I don't think it's something I need anymore. I have achieved what I set out to do, namely, finding a way through the impenetrable grief. Now I must live. In the past I didn't search out people to talk to, but today I feel it would be good to meet others who have been through the same things as I have, to be a vilomah, a parent who has lost a child. We are all survivors of something that goes against the natural order and sharing our stories of grief, loss and healing could be helpful to us all. I feel the need to let people know that it is okay, it is survivable. There is hope on the other side.

I will always think of you and keep you in my heart. I have no fear of death as I know it would mean seeing you again, but I won't go out looking for it as I want to be here to see my other two grow up and live a happy and long life. Knowing that I will see you again helps. You will always be in my heart, and never far from my thoughts.

Love,

Mommy x

Postscript

When I showed this book to the people closest to me and asked them about the events as I remembered them, a few said that their recollections were very different to mine. I realised that I had not heard what they were telling me at the time. My mind did not register their concern, nor did I understand their worry. Maybe I was protecting myself from something that I was not able to face. Sadi and Marga's viewpoints were so different that they deserve a mention. Sadi said she was very unnerved when she drove with Mario and César to the house before meeting up with me and the twins at the hotel in Mataro. She said Mario had acted strangely. He did not react or reply to César's questions and just stared at him. She also noted that the twins were not happy with him when he carried them. I thought that this was because they had not seen him.

She pointed out that they were fine with the rest of the family. She told me this again, years after the death of the twins. I remembered her telling me, but only vaguely. I must have blocked it out of my mind. It seems so strange. Sadi also reminded me of the times she went to the apartment in Hout Bay to help Mario with the kids. She said the twins were always unhappy to see her go and wanted to leave with her. It must have been hard on all of them.

Marga translated the first version of the book into Spanish so that my Spanish side of the family could read it. She also said she was not happy leaving the children with Mario. The first time she did so, Maximo clung to her leg. The second time they made her change into her pyjamas and sleep in their beds with them. They seemed to realise that she would be leaving them but thought that if Marga was in in bed with them it would mean that she would be staying. I am glad I do not remember that. It breaks my heart to realise that they were so miserable, maybe scared and needed Marga there, and that I did not do more to try and keep her there. All three kids must have suffered from the divorce. I did not see any signs of it. Perhaps it was another thing that I did not want to see. But I am glad I was reminded of it. It helped me realise how I did not listen and was not aware.

As I have said, there is no use in looking back to this time, I can do absolutely nothing to change that now. It is still painful. I try not to think of what I should or could have done, and what other outcomes would have been possible. I stop myself on the brink. There is no use. I can be perfectly fine, until I hear another version of events and the pain comes flooding back. It takes me by surprise. It lasts for a little while before I pull myself out of that hole, and remember the good times, their smiles and laughter. Their love. And my love for them.

PRECIOUS
MEMORIES

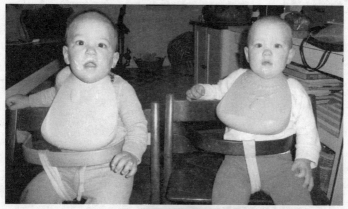

Top: Maximo and Octavia less than a year old

Left: Maximo and Octavia causing chaos in the kitchen

Below: The twins on Hout Bay Beach in South Africa

Top: Maximo and Octavia enjoying an ice cream with their big brother César

Left: Maximo and Octavia trying on my shoes

Below: César with his younger siblings

Top left:
Maximo and
Octavia geting
ready for a tree
top experience

Top right:
Maximo and
Octavia age one

Right: Maximo
and Octavia
riding their bikes
through a park

Books that helped me

Books have helped me heal and raised my awareness. I have gravitated towards books that empower self-healing, energy and meditation, which I realise may not be everyone's cup of tea, but we all have our own path to healing. Meditation is more accepted nowadays, and I hope more people take it up. There are so many different ways to do it, and just a few guidelines to follow. There are websites, blogs, apps, online courses and an infinite number of books.

Today, I continue to read every day and I invite you to take a look at some of the works that have had the greatest impact on me and my life. I believe these books can and should be read by anyone, no matter what trauma they've gone through – or haven't. There are useful lessons and ideas that can help everyone in any situation. It's difficult to summarise all of them to a paragraph but I have tried so as to give you an idea of how they have helped me. In truth, I could write essays on each book. I devoured each one, underlining countless sentences and earmarking many pages. I am so thankful for every word of them.

All these books and their inspiring words helped me in different areas, and I think they will help you a lot more than my story ever could.

If nothing else is taken from these pages I am grateful to be able to include a good reading list.

The Healing Code by Alexander Loyd.
The Book of Forgiving by Desmond Tutu
and Mpho Tutu.
The Book of Joy by the Dalai Lama
and Archbishop Desmond Tutu
Healing After Loss by Martha Whitmore Hickman
The Tao of Joy by Derek Lin
Radical Compassion by Tara Brach
Welcoming the Unwelcome by Pema Chödrön.
Love Out Loud by Nicole Gibson
Choosing Compassion by Anam Thubten.
When Breath becomes Air by Paul Kalanithi.

The following books are very different to the ones above, but in their own way helped me on my path to self-discovery:

Energy Medicine by Donna Eden and David Feinstein.
Beyond Willpower by Alex Lloyd
The Brain's Way of Healing by Norman Doidge
Breath by James Nestor
The Book You Wish Your Parents Had Read
by Philippa Perry
**A Course in Miracles Made Easy: Mastering the
Journey from Fear to Love** by Alan Cohen
The Soul of an Octopus by Sy Montgomery
My Octopus Teacher Netflix documentary